Beyond Baked Beans Green
REAL **VEGGIE** FOOD FOR **STUDENTS**

Absolute Press

Fiona Beckett

Beyond Baked Beans Green
REAL **VEGGIE** FOOD FOR **STUDENTS**

First published in Great Britain in 2004
by **Absolute Press**
Scarborough House
29 James Street West
Bath BA1 2BT
Phone 44 (0) 1225 316013
Fax 44 (0) 1225 445836
E-mail info@absolutepress.co.uk
Website www.absolutepress.co.uk

For more information visit
www.beyondbakedbeans.com

Publisher Jon Croft
Editor Meg Avent
Designer Matt Inwood

Illustrations by Andy Pedler
Research by Meg Devenish

A catalogue record of this book is available
from the British Library

ISBN 1 904573 14 2

Printed and bound by Lego, Italy

CONTENTS

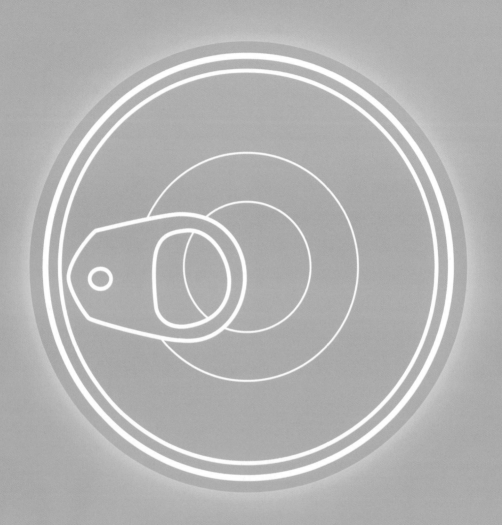

INTRO

This is not your average vegetarian cookery book. It's for veggies, of course – in particular for veggie students and other veggies on a restricted income but it's also for non-veggies too. I suppose that's not surprising given that I'm not a vegetarian myself but as is typical of many people nowadays often find myself choosing and cooking meatless – and fishless – meals. Like many families we've had children who have been vegetarian and one who still doesn't eat dairy, so it's become a familiar way of eating and one I very much enjoy.

What I don't like is a lot of what passes for veggie food. Meat substitutes for one so you won't find a lot about them in this book. I also find many veggie meals too heavy. Too often an excess of cheese makes up for the absence of meat. I was surprised to find how many of the recipes I came up with were vegan even though I didn't set out to make them so. That's certainly so in the case of my favourite vegetarian cuisines, Indian, Middle Eastern and Thai.

This book is also a bit different because I don't believe that students are incapable of doing more than opening a can of beans (hence the title). After all if you can study for a degree you can read a recipe. But just like everyone else there are times when you're in a rush and need to rustle up something quickly, others when you have to cook for a crowd and others when you want to push the boat out a bit. Which is why I've divided the recipes into three sections Solo, Sharing and Show-Off.

The big advantage of eating vegetarian (apart from the obvious benefit to the animal world) is that your diet is more likely to be a healthy one. It should also be less expensive though I do think veggies sometimes get ripped off on specialist products that should be cheaper than they are. But it's perfectly possible, as I hope you'll discover, to live on a student budget without in any way depriving yourself of delicious tasty food.

8 HOW NOT TO MISS MEAT

Unless you've been veggie all your life there's bound to be something you miss about meat. Whether it's the tantalising smell of bacon sandwiches, the family Sunday roast or a sizzling sausage straight off the barbecue there are times when your resolve may be tested. (Apologies to those of you who find these references offensive but it does hit some veggies hard.)

The good news is that it's perfectly possible to incorporate almost all of those textures and flavours in a veggie diet, and I don't just mean by meat substitutes. There are ingredients whose flavours are satisfyingly savoury and techniques for cooking that enhance the satisfaction of eating in just the same way as meat.

The taste sensation you need to seek out is *umami*, which has been identified as the fifth taste (along with sweet, sour, salty and bitter). It has a mouthwatering savouriness that you find in ingredients such as soy-based products, dried mushrooms, tomatoes, peas, Parmesan cheese, sesame oil and Marmite (especially when diluted as stock).

MAGIC MUSHROOMS (AND AUBERGINES)

No veggie diet would be worthwhile without mushrooms. The best type are the large dark portabella variety, which are wonderful baked with butter, garlic and parsley, or sliced up into a stew. Dried mushrooms (porcini) are also very useful for intensifying a dish's flavour. They're expensive but you don't need many. Aubergines are another super-veg, especially when roasted, grilled or combined, Japanese-style, with soy sauce, miso or sesame.

SAVOURY SPICES AND SEASONINGS

You can also enhance the savouriness of a dish by the spices and flavourings you use.

Essentials in my store cupboard are:

CHINESE FIVE SPICE POWDER
Combines with onions to give a rich, almost gravy-like flavour.

MARMITE
Ditto. I use it as a substitute for beef stocks.

SOY SAUCE
A must for stir-fries and as a substitute for fish sauce in savoury Asian style soups. Choose the light kind – it's more flexible.

SMOKED PIMENTON
A premium Spanish paprika with a really rich, filling flavour. Add it to tomato and pepper-based stews.

FRESH PARMESAN OR GRANA PADANO CHEESE
A worthwhile expense. Don't buy the pre-grated variety – it's a waste of money.

Also useful when you can afford them are:

BALSAMIC VINEGAR
Expensive but you need very little. Enriches salad dressings, and accentuates the flavours of tomatoes.

HOISIN SAUCE
A soy-based sweet and spicy barbecue sauce flavoured with star anise or five spice. Good with green veg like broccoli.

MISO
A rich soy bean paste that comes in light (white) and dark (brown or red) versions. The darker ones are more savoury and excellent as a base for vegetable soups and stews. Miso is also available in instant soup sachets – much, much tastier and more satisfying than Cup-a-Soup!

RED WINE
Many delicious meat-based stews and sauces are cooked with red wine. You can create a similar effect with mushroom stews. The longer you cook red wine, the more concentrated and flavourful it gets.

SEAWEED (DRIED)
Has a chewy, salty, savouriness that somehow makes up for meat. The two best types to go for are nori, the kind you find wrapped around sushi, and konbu, which is the basis of the Japanese stock dashi (which also contains dried tuna flakes, which rules it out if you're a veggie). You can toast sheets of nori lightly over a flame, then cut it into thin strips and scatter it over noodles or a soup. (Or simply use the deep-fried 'seaweed' you get in some supermarket takeaways.)

SESAME SEEDS AND OIL
Toast the seeds in a dry frying pan to enhance their nuttiness. With the oil you literally need a few drops to give a pervasive rich nutty flavour to stir- fries and salads.

SUNDRIED TOMATOES
Sun-drying accentuates tomatoes' natural *umami* (see p8). Buy them in packets and reconstitute them with warm water – they taste sweeter and more natural than the ones in oil.

FLAVOUR-ENHANCING COOKING TECHNIQUES

If you think about it what you probably used to find most appealing about meat was the way it was cooked – that yummy caramelised effect you get from high temperature cooking such as roasting, grilling and barbecuing. Well, you can get a similar effect by roasting, grilling, searing and barbecuing vegetables. Even slow cooking can bring out flavour in a very satisfying way – just think of slow braised onions which get richer, darker and sweeter the longer you cook them. Same with tomatoes – slow roast them and you get something deliciously chewy and satisfying. Giving a dish a crispy topping whether you use cheese or breadcrumbs to do it also makes a dish taste crunchier and more appetising.

10 THE ART AND SCIENCE OF SHOPPING

Knowing how to shop is just as important as knowing how to cook, especially if you're on a tight budget. You might wonder why. Surely, shopping is perfectly straightforward – you go to the supermarket. You buy what you want. You come home and cook – or just eat it. But supermarkets don't make huge profits for nothing. Their aim in life is to make you spend more than you planned – seducing you through their doors with special offers, then cunningly sneaking in hidden price rises on the things you buy routinely like bog roll or bananas. So long as you're aware of that, no problem, but what you need are the seemingly contradictory skills of planning ahead and being prepared to change your mind.

An example. It's November and you go into your local supermarket expecting to buy the ingredients for a roast vegetable pasta. But the price of aubergines, courgettes and peppers has gone through the roof (not so surprising – they're right out of season). There is however a really good offer on frozen peppers so you could use them instead. Root veg are also cheap this week, particularly if you buy them loose (always cheaper than buying them pre-packed) so you decide to buy some for a root vegetable roast the next day and extra carrots for a soup. You also take advantage of the 3 for the price of 2 offer on own-brand pasta which will mean you don't have to buy any for the next month.

It takes time to think this way, I admit. It's useful to have some idea of what you might make, otherwise you just wander the aisles picking up things at random without knowing what you're going to do with them. But be prepared to change your mind in the light of what you find. And check the shelf tags carefully.

Supermarkets, of course, aren't the only place to buy your food – like all other shops, they're good for some things and less good for others. And if you want smaller, more individual shops to survive it's important to give them your custom.

WHERE TO SHOP

SUPERMARKETS
Good for: store cupboard staples like tea, coffee, pasta, tinned tomatoes, tinned pulses, frozen veg, packet salads and stir-fries, ready-meals, pizza.
Bad for: fresh produce, especially herbs, can be expensive. So can spices, specialist breads like pitta bread or ciabatta, nuts and dried fruits.

SPECIALIST FOOD SHOPS
(Such as bakers, greengrocers and cheese shops)
Good for: high quality products that you won't find elsewhere like good wholemeal loaves, real farmhouse cheeses, great olives and locally sourced veg.
You also get to talk to someone who knows about the product. **Bad for:** prices, which tend to be higher than in the supermarket though not invariably so.

ETHNIC SHOPS

(Such as Asian and Middle Eastern grocers, Italian delis, Chinese supermarkets)

Good for: fresh herbs such as parsley, mint and coriander (much cheaper than supermarkets), spices and seasonings such as garlic and ginger, rice and dal, exotic fruits and veg such as okra and mangoes, any ingredients in which that country specialises e.g. Parmesan, Feta and Mozzarella cheese, soy sauce, sesame oil and sweet chilli sauce. **Bad for:** staples such as coffee or tea.

HEALTH FOOD SHOPS AND CO-OPERATIVES

Good for: nuts, dried fruits, pulses and grains, good quality tofu, sprouting seeds and specialist vegan products. **Bad for:** fresh fruit and veg tend to be pricey (and not always as fresh as they might be). So are ingredients such as honey and other spreads.

MARKETS

(Street markets, farmers markets, WI markets)

Good for: very cheap fruit and veg, especially towards the end of the day (street markets), locally grown organic veg, eggs and cheese (farmers markets), locally grown veg and home-baked cakes, pies and jams (W1 markets). **Bad for:** you need to watch the quality, especially with street markets. Try and pick the produce yourself.

VEG BOX SCHEMES:

Good for: cheap seasonal veg. **Bad for:** can go to waste if you don't plan how to use it when it arrives.

UNI SHOPS

Good for emergency supplies of storecupboard staples you've run out of. Like tea. **Bad for** choice and price on almost everything else.

WHAT TO BUY

WHAT YOU NEED IN YOUR STORE CUPBOARD (OR FRIDGE)

Obviously no student these days has a budget for a huge storecupboard full of food but it does make sense to have enough to hand to be able to knock up a meal at short notice without having to shop. And if you want an interesting meal you need to build on that. Not everyone of course wants the same thing – some people live on pasta, others prefer rice and noodles. Still others wouldn't want any animal-derived products, but here are the basics I would want to have to hand. Buy them as and when you can afford them.

A COUPLE OF ONIONS
A JAR OF TINNED TOMATOES OR A CARTON OF PASSATA OR CREAMED TOMATOES
A PACK OF DRIED SPAGHETTI OR OTHER PASTA SHAPES preferably Italian
SOME BASIC COOKING OIL sunflower or rapeseed for preference
A BOTTLE OF INEXPENSIVE OLIVE OIL for salad dressings
RED OR WHITE WINE VINEGAR (ditto)
A JAR OF DIJON MUSTARD (ditto)

12 THE ART AND SCIENCE OF SHOPPING

FINE SEA SALT
A PEPPER GRINDER FILLED WITH BLACK
PEPPERCORNS
MARIGOLD VEGETABLE (OR VEGAN)
BOUILLON POWDER
  Far better than most stock cubes for soups or stock.
A PACK OF BASMATI RICE
  Much more flavour than the easy-cook kind.
A SELECTION OF TINNED PULSES
  Such as chickpeas, lentils, red kidney beans
  and cannellini beans.
PLAIN UNSWEETENED YOGHURT
  To accompany fresh fruit or stir into dips,
  dressings or curries.
A JAR OF RUNNY HONEY For drizzling over
  yoghurt and fresh fruit or simply as a spread.
HALF A DOZEN EGGS Do buy free-range.
A PACK OF CHEDDAR OR OTHER HARD
  CHEESE
SOME CHERRY TOMATOES
A PACK OF FROZEN PEAS

Not to mention coffee, tea, sugar (preferably
unrefined) fresh and long-life milk, bread, breakfast
cereal, some kind of butter or low-fat spread, and
a selection of fresh fruit.

NEAR-ESSENTIALS

If you want to produce food that's exciting as well as
edible you'll also need (and I wouldn't be without):

A HEAD OF GARLIC
  Keep in the cupboard rather than the fridge.
ONE OR TWO LEMONS
  Preferably unwaxed which means you can use
  the rind as well as the juice.
A LIME (Again, unwaxed.)
SOME FRESH PARSLEY AND/OR CORIANDER
  Buy it from an Asian or Middle Eastern grocer –
  the bunches are twice the size and half the price
  of those you find in supermarkets.
A JAR OF MOROCCAN SPICE MIX
  A mild, aromatic blend and the mix I use most
  regularly for recipes. Make up a batch from:
  2 tbsp ground cumin, 2 tbsp ground coriander,
  1 tbsp turmeric and 1-2 tsp chilli powder or hot
  pimenton (see p 8). Blend well and use as
  desired (about 2 tsp at a time).
WHOLE CUMIN SEEDS
  For adding extra flavour to eastern Mediterranean,
  Middle Eastern and Indian recipes. Put them in
  a dry (i.e. unoiled) frying pan and warm them
  gently until they change colour and give off a
  spicy aroma. Then cool and crush them lightly.
MILD CHILLI POWDER If you're into chilli.
GARAM MASALA A rich sweet Indian spice
  mix – good with lentils.

DRIED OREGANO OR HERBES DE PROVENCE
For giving sauces and pasta dishes that authentic Mediterranean flavour.
DRIED THYME Suits plain British cooking, shepherd's pie, roast root veg.
SOY SAUCE Light, rather than dark.
SWEET CHILLI SAUCE
Use as a dipping sauce or as an alternative to ketchup.
FRESH GINGER OR GINGER PASTE Adds a hot lemony kick to stir-fries and other Asian dishes. Buy a chunk, keep it wrapped in the fridge, then peel and grate it as you need it.
PLUS THE INGREDIENT'S LISTED IN *HOW NOT TO MISS MEAT* (See p9.)

A FEW OTHER THINGS THAT MIGHT BE USEFUL

A JAR OF MAYONNAISE For salads and sandwiches.
A PACK OF INSTANT MASH Flakes rather than powder.
A JAR OF PEANUT BUTTER
For those who aren't allergic to nuts, obviously. Good for sandwiches, dips or dressings.
SOME GOOD QUALITY JAPANESE INSTANT NOODLES
A FEW NUTS, SEEDS AND SOME DRIED FRUIT TO NIBBLE (See Power Snacks, pp22-23.)

NOT STRICTLY VEGGIE

If you've only just become a vegetarian you may not be aware that many products you assume are veggie or vegan aren't so at all. Like cheeses which contain rennet or wines and beers that have been fined with egg white or isinglass. That often means that ready-meals or cook-in sauces that contain cheese may not be veggie even if they're based on vegetables. Thai green and red curry sauce, to give another example, sound as if they should be suitable for vegetarians but many contain fish sauce and shrimp paste. Many common products such as crisps, biscuits, chocolate and even stock powder contain whey powder which is unacceptable to vegans. Fortunately most supermarket products are well labelled – it's harder to know what you're getting with branded goods and when you're eating out. For a comprehensive list of pitfalls to avoid log on to the Vegetarian Society's comprehensive list on www.vegsoc.org/info/stumbling.html.

14   KIT

There isn't a big difference in the kit you need in your kitchen if you're a veggie. I'd say a wok was more important – you'll probably do more stir-fries than the average meat-eater – and a hand held blender, maybe. You'll probably make more soups.

Far more important is the stage you're at at uni, where you're living, and at what age you go there. Someone who is 19 and living in their first year in hall is going to use a lot less stuff than someone who's gone back to uni when they're 25. Or who is mad keen on baking.

So I've attempted to draw up a list for each stage of uni. If it seems like a daunting one, remember not everything has to be new, or acquired at the same time. Your parents will probably be more than willing to offload old toasters, kettles and saucepans (gives them an excuse to buy new ones!), and you can easily pick up plates, cutlery and glasses in charity shops. Most supermarkets also now have a 'budget' range of pans and other equipment, as do Woolworths and IKEA. So go and have a browse.

IN HALL

A shared kitchen and limited storage space means keeping equipment to a minimum. Appliances like kettles and microwaves should be laid on. Most of your cooking will probably take place on top of the stove, **so all you should really need is:**

A WOK
Probably more useful to you than a frying pan unless you live off fry-ups (as if!). Metal ones are cheaper but need rinsing and drying carefully after use, otherwise they can rust. So probably not for you then.

A LARGE SAUCEPAN OR STEAMER.
The main purpose of which will probably be to cook pasta or rice, but it can also be used for soup. The advantage of steamers – which are not too expensive these days – is that they have an in-built colander which means you can strain the pasta when you've finished cooking it. And steam veggies too.

A SMALL/MEDIUM NON-STICK PAN
For scrambling eggs, making gravy, heating up beans or soup.

A CHOPPING BOARD
Plastic is easier to clean – and cheaper.

A SMALL KITCHEN KNIFE
For preparing vegetables.

A PAIR OF SCISSORS
For opening those plastic packets you can't open with anything else. You may already have some for work which will do.

A CAN OPENER
Not all cans have ring pulls.

A CORKSCREW
Get an old-fashioned 'twist and pull' one. Plastic corks will destroy a decent one.

A WOODEN SPOON
Preferably two.

A FISH SLICE OR SPATULA
Not for fish, but for lifting fried eggs or anything else flat and floppy out of a frying pan or wok.

A GRATER
For cheese (Cheddar on the large holes, Parmesan on the small ones), carrots, fresh ginger. The square box-style type is easier to use.

A SMALL MIXING BOWL
For mixing up salad dressings (unless you have a convenient jam jar), beating eggs, etc.

A MEASURING JUG
Graded with solid measurements as well as liquid ones.

MEASURING SPOONS
Not vital but they're not expensive and do make following recipes easier.

A PEPPER MILL
Freshly ground pepper makes a world of difference (see p12). It doesn't have to be one of those flashy wooden ones – a plastic one will do fine.

A GARLIC CRUSHER
Quicker and less smelly than chopping by hand.

A COUPLE OF CHEAP PLASTIC BOXES
For storing leftovers in the fridge.

And for your wish list:

A HAND-HELD BLENDER
Mainly for blitzing soups. Some have attachments for chopping up nuts and herbs, a whisk for beating eggs or cream and a blender for smoothies.

A STUDENT HOUSE

You're more likely to have an oven or, more to the point, more likely to want to use it.

So, add these to your list:

A LARGE ROASTING DISH
For roast veggies and pasta bakes.

A MEDIUM-SIZED MICROWAVEABLE DISH
Obviously essential if you have a microwave. But it should do double duty in a convential oven if you want to make a crumble for example. Or something like a macaroni cheese.

A BAKING SHEET
Useful for heating up pizzas and cooking pies and cookies. If you're into baking get two.

You could also add to your collection of pans:

A MEDIUM TO LARGE NON-STICK FRYING PAN
AN EXTRA MEDIUM-SIZED SAUCEPAN
For cooking veggies.

A SMALL METAL PAN
For boiling eggs (boiling water tends to wreck a non-stick surface over time).

You might also want to think about:

A COLANDER AND/OR A SIEVE
If you don't have a steamer you'll need something to strain your pasta (you can also use it as a steamer if you fit it on top of a saucepan and

cover it with a lid). A sieve is useful for rice or for straining lumpy sauces.

A LARGE MIXING BOWL

Will double as a salad bowl.

SCALES

Depends how precisely you like to measure things. If buying some try to get electronic ones that measure to the nearest gram.

A TIMER

Unless you're amazingly well organised.

A SERRATED BREAD KNIFE

If you're into unsliced bread. Quite useful for cutting tomatoes too.

A LEMON SQUEEZER

You can stick a fork in the cut side of half a lemon and wiggle it while you squeeze but you'll get more juice out of a squeezer.

A VEGETABLE PEELER

Not essential but it does make the job easier.

A POTATO MASHER

Ditto. Worth getting if you're heavily into mash

A CHEESE SLICER

Yes, you can use a knife, but a slicer makes it much easier to cut fine slices for sandwiches and as a topping for toast.

AN ICE-TRAY

Certainly if you're into cocktails. Nice for cold drinks during exam time too.

A LARGE JUG

Also for mixing cocktails or – more likely, of course – soft drinks.

A BISCUIT TIN

To stop your biscuits going soggy.

Put on your wish list:

A PESTLE AND MORTAR

Good for some Jamie-style bashing. Useful if you're into Thai, Indian or Moroccan cooking – anything which involves grinding up spices. Fun to use too. You'll find them cheapest in Asian supermarkets.

THE MATURE STUDENT/ ENTHUSIASTIC COOK

If you're cooking regularly you will want slightly better quality kitchen tools than when you first started. Look for bargains in discount stores such as TK Maxx or department stores during the sales and upgrade your pans as and when you can afford to. Obviously you'll need more equipment if you're living on your own than you will sharing, but you can always borrow from your friends if you're cooking up a feast.

Other kit you might want to add:

A CAST-IRON GRILL PAN

A heavyweight ridged grill pan for quick, low-fat cooking. Get the grill really hot (about 3-4 minutes on the hob), lightly smear or spray your food with oil then quickly sear it either side. Gives a real barbecue flavour – but creates a lot of smoke. . (See GMVs p52).

A ROTARY WHISK

If you want to whip cream or egg whites for meringues. An electric one is, of course, easier.

For basic whisking (e.g. eggs, salad dressings) a fork will do.
A ROLLING PIN
If you want to make or roll out pastry.
2 x SMALL ROUND CAKE TINS
If you want to make a layered cake (see p150).
A LOAF TIN FOR A SIMPLE SLICING CAKE
(See p151.)
A MUFFIN PAN
(See p149) Also for Yorkshire puddings (see p93).
A SHALLOW RECTANGULAR BAKING TIN
For flapjacks (see p 146).
BAKING PARCHMENT
To stop your cakes sticking.
SOME CLEAN JAM JARS
For sprouting seeds (see p28).

Put on your wish list:

A FOOD PROCESSOR
Takes the hard grind out of making pastry, pureeing pulses (see Lebanese-style Lentil Cake, p84, and Spicy Beanburgers, p85), and chopping ingredients like vegetables and nuts.
A COFFEE MAKER
Real coffee is an expensive habit but once you've got the bug nothing else will do. It doesn't need to be electric, though. Go for a cafetiere if you like a lighter style coffee, an Italian stove-top coffee pot if you want a strong espresso hit.

OTHER KITCHEN BASICS

FOIL, CLING FILM, SOME ROBUST RUBBER BANDS (for putting round packets once you open them), KITCHEN TOWEL, SOME PLASTIC BAGS (for keeping fresh herbs in), OVEN GLOVES, AN APRON, PLASTERS (for when you inevitably cut yourself), A FIRE BLANKET OR EXTINGUISHER (just in case), WASHING-UP LIQUID, SCOURERS/ WASHING-UP BRUSH, TEA-TOWELS (enough to always have a clean one....), SPONGE CLOTHS, KITCHEN CLEANER, BRILLO PADS (for stuck-on gunk but no good for non-stick pans), BIN BAGS, A FRIDGE THERMOMETER (to tell if your fridge is cold enough. Obviously, turn it up if it isn't).

AND FOR THE TABLE...

FORKS, KNIVES, SPOONS, TEASPOONS, SERVING SPOONS, LARGE PLATES, SIDE PLATES, MUGS (vast quantities of), EGG CUPS, SOUP/CEREAL BOWLS, AND A COUPLE OF SERVING PLATES/BOWLS.

WHAT YOU NEED TO EAT (AND AVOID)

You might think as a veggie that you have a well-balanced diet and that may well be true. But it's just as easy to eat unhealthily as a vegetarian or a vegan as a meat eater. You also have the added drawback that you may be missing out on certain vital vitamins and minerals. Since some foods are also ruled out on grounds of expense, it's particularly important to balance those you can afford so you get the nutrients you need from a variety of food sources.

FRUIT AND VEG

We're constantly urged to eat at least five portions of fruit and veg a day in order to get the essential vitamins, minerals and fibre we need. Although it's not easy, for a veggie it's vital. The trick is to try and incorporate some kind of fruit or veg in every meal – a glass of fruit juice with breakfast, a tomato in your lunchtime sarnie, an apple or banana as an afternoon snack, a mushroom omelette and a salad for your evening meal and you're there. What counts as a portion isn't so dauntingly huge. A couple of plums, a slice of melon or pineapple, a small salad or three heaped tablespoons of any fresh, tinned or frozen vegetable (that's about six mouthfuls). Pulses like beans or lentils count too, though only once a day. The important thing is to vary them. It wouldn't be clever to have 5 daily helpings of cucumber for instance. Some fruit and veg are especially good for us – green leafy vegetables like broccoli (an important source of beta-carotene, folate and vitamin C) and kiwi fruit and strawberries (both also high in vitamin C – see opposite). Organic fruit and veg contain more nutrients than non-organic ones.

CARBOHYDRATES

With all the hype about the Atkins diet carbohydrates like bread and pasta have been getting a bad press lately, but as they're both cheap and filling they've always formed the basis of the student diet. They still should – you need complex carbs as a source of energy and fibre. The crucial thing is not to combine them with loads of fat. Don't overdo the chips or weigh down your baked potatoes with vast amounts of cheese. Good sources are meals based on pasta, rice, beans and lentils and on wholemeal bread. Again vary them. Try wholewheat versions which have more fibre and give you more sustained energy (see eating for exams p23). You also get carbs from fruit and veg so you're quids in there.

PROTEIN

We need protein for cell renewal and repair – to keep our bodies functioning. Vegetarians and particularly vegans have to make more of a conscious effort than meat eaters to incorporate it into their diet, but you don't need much (about 45g a day for women, and 55g for men) and there are plenty of alternative sources including eggs, cheese, milk, yoghurt, beans, lentils, nuts, seeds, soy-based products like tofu and fortified cereals. There are also some surpising sources such as peas and green vegetables such as spinach and sprouts. There's some dispute as to whether you need to combine these ingredients with carbohydrate to make what's called a 'complete protein', as in hummus and pitta bread, rice and dal, or beans on toast. It certainly won't do any harm and it's probably the way you're most likely to eat them anyway.

FAT

Fat is not all bad (it keeps you warm and helps you to absorb vital vitamins). However, it's better to confront it in the form of upfront, obvious fat than the hidden sneaky fats you find in cakes, biscuits and snack foods such as crisps. Nutritionists distinguish between less healthy saturated fats – the kind you find in dairy products, and more virtuous unsaturated ones like olive oil and the oil you find in nuts and avocados.

VITAMINS AND MINERALS

Especially important for vegans who don't have the option of getting them from animal products. But there are perfectly good alternative sources.

IRON

Crucially important for women who can otherwise be drained by their monthly periods and become anaemic, tired and lacking in energy. Good sources are: fortified breakfast cereals, lentils, chickpeas, green leafy vegetables such as spinach, dried apricots, pumpkin seeds, sesame seeds, soya mince and nuts. Consuming a food or drink rich in vitamin C with an iron-rich food – like a glass of orange juice with a bowl of cereal, or lentils with a tomato sauce (see p40) – helps the body to absorb iron.

CALCIUM

The most obvious source of calcium, which you need for strong bones and teeth, are dairy foods such as milk, cheese and yoghurt. If you don't eat them, you can get what you need from tofu, fortified soya milk, green leafy vegetables such as broccoli and cabbage, sesame seeds, chickpeas, and even good old baked beans! Even if you do eat dairy products it's good to get some of your calcium from these sources.

VITAMIN B12

The B vitamins are responsible for keeping you cheery and sane but the particularly important B12, is found only in animal products. Vegetarians can get it from eggs, milk and cheese, but vegans should include Marmite, and fortified breakfast cereals, soy products and spreads in their diet (check the label).

VITAMIN C

Vital to keep your immune system functioning properly and build up resistance to stress. What you absorb may be depleted faster if you're a smoker. Boost your intake by eating and drinking more foods that are vitamin C rich such as oranges, kiwi fruit, strawberries and fresh peppers. Better still, give up smoking!

For more information about what you should be eating and why, log on to the Food Standard Agency website at www.foodstandards.gov.uk/healthiereating/

20 A HEALTHY DAY'S EATING

It's easy to be daunted by the idea of healthy eating. To think that unless you have three proper meals a day you aren't eating properly. But today's fast-paced lifestyle, let alone the student lifestyle doesn't make that easy. What you need to do is supplement the meals you do have time to make with some creative snacking.

You can at least start with a good breakfast. Or indeed any breakfast. It doesn't have to be a cooked one. A bowl of fortified cereal, a banana, some orange juice and coffee would do. If you won't eat again for a few hours grab a mid-morning snack – an unsweetened cereal bar, a yoghurt, or an apple. At lunchtime try to have something that will sustain you through the afternoon. If you're out, a wholemeal bap, wrap or sandwich, with hummus and roast veg or with cheese and tomato, for example. If you're studying at home, some home-made soup, bread and cheese or scrambled eggs on wholemeal toast with mushrooms, would be great. Accompany it with a glass of fruit juice or a piece of fruit to follow.

If hunger strikes mid-afternoon have – hell, why not? – a muffin or a piece of cake. Eating isn't supposed to be purgatory. In the evening, a stir-fry with nuts or tofu, or a plate of pasta and salad and some fruit should see you through. If you eat early – or go to bed late – top up with a snack before bedtime to help you sleep and prevent night-time hunger pangs. At 3 a.m. in the morning, a bowl of cereal is better than a bag of chips.

FOUR THINGS TO REMEMBER

1 TRY NOT TO SKIP MEALS
If you do, make up for it with a power snack (see p22). Don't go for hours without eating – or drinking. It's important to have at least 2 litres of fluid a day – not including booze (see p23).

2 VARY YOUR DIET
It's easy to get into a rut once you've mastered a couple of recipes but try not to eat the same thing everyday. This will let you incorporate a variety of different foods into your diet. (Obviously it's OK to eat the same ingredient a couple of days running to use it up, but try to vary the way you eat it.)

3 STOCK UP WITH HEALTHY FOODS
When you do go to the supermarket or local shops, stock up with healthy, fresh foods. If the only thing to hand is a packet of microwave chips and a pack of biscuits, that's what you'll eat.

4 EATING IS SOCIAL
Aim for at least a couple of meals during the week where you do cook properly from scratch and sit down round a table with your housemates or friends. Sunday lunch or dinner, for example.

QUICK IDEAS FOR
HEALTHY BREAKFASTS

- Crunchy Brown Sugar and Cinnamon Porridge (see p70), plus some orange or apple juice
- Apple and Raisin Muesli (see p72)
- Strawberry Roughie (see p73)
- Scrambled eggs on wholewheat toast

QUICK IDEAS FOR
WINTER LUNCHES

- A bowl of soup (like the Italian Bean and Pasta Soup on p38, or the lovely Leek and Potato Soup on p58), plus a slice of wholemeal bread plus a chunk of cheese
- Pan-fried Cheese and Onion Toastie (see p62) and a salad
- Quick Buttered Vegetable Pasta (see p43)
- All Seasons Pasta Salad (see p45)

QUICK IDEAS FOR
WINTER SUPPERS

- Basque Butterbean Stew (see p36)
- Broccoli, Chilli and Garlic Pasta (see p44)
- Simple Stir-fry with Cashew Nuts (see p46)
- Carrot and Lentil Pilau (see p96) plus a veggie curry

QUICK IDEAS FOR
SUMMER LUNCHES

- GMVs with Hummus and Pitta Bread (see p52)
- Cheese, Celery and Apple Salad with Yoghurt and Honey Dressing (see p54)
- Mixed Bean and Crumbly White Cheese Salad (see p55)
- Surprisingly Good Spring Onion and Beansprout Omelette (see p66)

QUICK IDEAS FOR
SUMMER SUPPERS

- Summer Spaghetti with Cherry Tomatoes and Goats' Cheese (see p41)
- Marinated Tofu with Quick Spicy Beansprout Salad (see p47)
- Moroccan Spiced Chickpeas and Spinach (see p38)
- Veggie Burgers and Black Eye Bean Salsa (see p39)

WHAT MAKES A DIRE DAY'S EATING

No breakfast. Black coffee at midday. A couple of pints and a cheese and onion pasty at the pub. A couple of chocolate bars in the afternoon, washed down with a couple of mugs of sweetened tea. A large deep-dish, four-cheese pizza. (No salad or veg.) Four more pints of beer and/or several `vodkas. More black coffee.

Snacking has a bad name but it actually suits the student lifestyle. And many other modern lifestyles, for that matter. You don't always have time for a proper meal and the longer you leave it before you eat, the more likely you are to stuff yourself with empty calories. What you need is a stock of healthy snacks that can address deficiencies in your diet like a lack of calcium or iron. **Prepare to power snack**.

Note: Many of these snacks will give you a boost in more ways than one, e.g. Brie will contribute protein and calcium to your diet, grapes contain potassium, which is good for regulating your body's sodium (salt) intake and blood pressure. All solid snacks are best accompanied with some kind of liquid, preferably water.

PROTEIN BOOSTERS

- A hard boiled egg, a few cherry tomatoes and a stick of cucumber or celery
- A small chunk of Cheddar* or Stilton*, a couple of oatcakes or a few walnuts and an apple
- A small chunk of Brie* and a few grapes or cherries
- A small low-fat yoghurt* and some fresh berries, (strawberries or raspberries)
- A glass of semi-skimmed milk* or soy milk (made into a milk shake or cocoa if you don't like milk)
- A smoothie* or a roughie* (see p73)

* these products also boost calcium

MINERAL BOOSTERS

- Any of the aforementioned snacks marked *
- A handful of dried apricots (iron and potassium), and a few mixed nuts
- A few brazil nuts (vitamin E, selenium, zinc and iron) and a chunk of fresh mango
- A handful of roast peanuts in their shells – so long as you're not allergic to peanuts (zinc)
- A bowl of fortified breakfast cereal

VITAMIN BOOSTERS

- A couple of satsumas or clementines (vitamin C)
- 2-3 ripe fresh apricots (vitamin A)
- A fresh peach (vitamin C)
- A kiwi fruit, crispbread and a couple of spoonfuls of cottage cheese (vitamin C)
- Some raw vegetable strips (e.g. peppers, celery, carrot) with Hummus or Gado Gado dip (see p74) – vitamins A and C
- Wholemeal toast and Marmite (vitamin B)
- A mug of miso soup (vitamin B12)
- Plain tortilla chips and Fresh Tomato Salsa (see p75) (vitamin C)
- Half an avocado with a spoonful of salad dressing (vitamin E)
- A mixed grain crispbread spread with soft cheese or hummus and topped with sprouting seeds (see p28) (vitamin C)

ENERGY BOOSTERS

These complex carbs will keep you going.
- A couple of oatcakes and cream cheese or honey
- A low sugar cereal bar or sesame snap
- A banana sandwich made with wholemeal bread plus a few dates or raisins
- A wholewheat pitta bread with peanut butter, grated carrot, apple and lemon juice

LIQUID HEALTH

It's vital to keep your fluid intake up.
The recommended amount is 2 litres a day. That should mainly be water but as veggies you should also drink 2-3 small glasses of fruit juice, such as orange juice, apple juice or cranberry juice (all unsweetened) to help absorb other nutrients. If you're vegan or dairy-intolerant a couple of glasses of calcium-enriched water or fruit juice would also help.

EATING FOR EXAMS

During exams it's even more crucial to eat properly. Lack of food (a skipped breakfast) or the wrong kind of eating (high-fat and/or sugary snacks) can play havoc with your blood sugar levels, giving you a short term boost but leaving you lacking in energy and unable to concentrate. Stress also depletes the amount of vitamin B and C in your body which in turn can leave you prone to depression and feeling you just can't cope.
If you aren't already eating fairly sensibly try and improve your routine in the run up to exams. Before a morning exam eat a good breakfast – porridge or muesli are ideal, plus, if you can face it, a boiled egg or cheese on wholemeal toast. The same prescription at lunchtime – complex carbs with a bit of protein – will keep you going through an afternoon exam. Beans on wholemeal toast, a wholemeal pitta bread or wrap with grilled veggies and hummus, or a good-sized portion of bean or chickpea salad would do the job. Exams certainly aren't the moment to worry about your weight – or about your budget. Spend a little extra on the odd ready-meal to take the pressure off. (Buy one from your local supermarket's healthy-eating range, and eat some extra veggies or a salad with it.) When you do find time to cook make enough for two meals.

LEARN TO LOVE THE VEG YOU LOATHE

...OR HAVEN'T EVEN TRIED.

A lot of food likes and dislikes are psychological. You think you don't like something because you don't like the sound of it or the look of it. Or because you can't imagine what it's going to taste like. Or you tried it once and didn't like it. If your only experience of sprouts, for example, was a sodden, yellowy-green vegetable that had been boiled for 30 minutes it wouldn't be surprising if you turned your back on them. The two main enemies of vegetables are water and overcooking.

A healthy veggie diet depends on variety, however, so it's as well to see if you can find a way of learning to like the veg you loathe (or think you loathe). I've left out innocuous, inoffensive veg like potatoes, peas, sweetcorn, lettuce, tomatoes and cucumber as most people like them. And I'm not sure I can help if you don't.

ASPARAGUS
Some people don't like the grassiness of asparagus, most pronounced when it's boiled or steamed. Try cooking it for $3^1/_2$ minutes in the microwave (see p36), then tossing it in a little olive oil and searing it for a minute on a very hot ridged grill pan, or dry (i.e. not oiled) frying pan. Serve with crumbled goats' cheese, or some thin slices of Parmesan cheese.

AUBERGINES
Can be slightly bitter and also, if not cooked briskly enough, oil-laden and soggy. If you have time salt them before you use them. (Cut the aubergine into cubes or slices, sprinkle generously with salt, leave for 30 minutes, rinse under running water then pat dry with kitchen towel.) Stir-fry quickly over a high heat and serve with a garlicky tomato sauce and a good handful of chopped coriander or parsley. They taste good as a salad too (see p118).

BEANS (BAKED)
My sympathies but try the recipe on p37.

BEANS (GREEN)
Need some kind of lubrication. Once you've cooked them (for about 5 minutes in boiling, salted water), drain and rinse them under cold running water. Heat a little butter (or oil and crushed garlic) in the pan you used for cooking them, return them to the pan, stir and heat through for a minute or two. Season with salt and pepper.

BEETROOT

Avoid the type with vinegar. Roast rather than boil them to get their full earthy sweetness. Buy them by the bunch in season (summer), trim off the leaves, rinse and dry them, wrap them individually in lightly oiled foil and bake them in a hot (200C/400F/Gas 6) oven for about 50 minutes to an hour. Cool, peel off the skins, and cut into wedges or slice. Great with a dark green salad and goats' cheese or a crumbly white cheese like Caerphilly or Wensleydale.

BROCCOLI

Best steamed for about 5 minutes. (Cut the florets off the stalk first and divide them into even-sized pieces.) You can also microwave them with a little water, or stir-fry them using the cabbage method (see right) with some soy or hoisin sauce.

BUTTERNUT SQUASH

The tough outer skin may be what's putting you off but take a large sharp knife and cut across the squash lengthways from top to bottom and scoop out the seeds. Cut into wedges, drizzle with oil, season generously with salt and a few crushed chillies, and roast in a hot oven (200C/400F/Gas 6) for 40-45 minutes. (see also Butternut Squash Risotto p113).

CABBAGE AND OTHER GREENS

Two solutions: either cook fast in a very little water, drain, add a good chunk of butter and season generously with pepper and a little salt. Or stir-fry in hot oil adding a little water and 1-2 tbsp of soy sauce (depending how much cabbage you're cooking). The latter method works better with strong dark greens like spring greens and kale. Either way thickly slice the leaves first, cutting away any tough bits of stalk.

CARROTS

If you don't like cooked carrots try them raw – grated as a salad or with a dip (see p74) – or briefly cooked as part of a stir-fry (see pp46-47). They're also very good roasted, along with other root veg such as onions and parsnips (see p92) and make fantastic soup (see p59).

CAULIFLOWER

Best steamed like broccoli (you can then smother it with cheese sauce!) or as part of a dry Indian-style curry (see Spiced Cauliflower and Potato on p94). And try the amazing Luxury Caramelised Cauliflower Soup on p130 – guaranteed to convert any cauliflower-hater.

CELERY

Just chop it up small and add to stews and pasta sauces when you soften the onion. You won't notice it's there. Or try raw fennel (much tastier) instead.

26 LEARN TO LIKE THE VEG YOU LOATHE

COURGETTES

Don't let water anywhere near them – they go disgustingly soggy. The best way to cook them is to grill them (see GMVs, p52) or to grate them and stir-fry them which literally takes a few seconds. (Grate the courgettes, heat a frying pan add a good lump of butter or a couple of tablespoons of oil, tip in the courgettes and stir-fry for a minute). Try the gorgeous Greek-style Potato, Courgette and Feta Bake too (p121).

GARLIC

As a garlic groupie I find it hard to believe that there's anyone in the world who doesn't share my passion. For those of you who don't, the secret – as with onions – is to cook it for a long time till it becomes deliciously sweet and caramelised. (See Roast Root Veg with Garlic and Rosemary p92). Also make sure your garlic isn't too elderly otherwise it will taste bitter. If it's yellowy and soft or has a green shoot growing out of the top, bin it!

LEEKS

Make great soup (see p58) and are a good substitute for spring onions in stir fries or with beans (see leek and lemon beans – p37). Also brilliant with eggs (try the goats' cheese and leek frittata on p67). You need to prepare them carefully though, otherwise they can be gritty. Trim off any roots and the coarse green leaves off the top of the leek (about a quarter of the way down). Slice thickly in rounds then wash thoroughly under running water. Don't on any account boil them.

MUSHROOMS

If there's one veg you really, really should learn to love as a veggie it's mushrooms. They come in all shapes and sizes so it should be possible to find one type that appeals. Try them raw for a start. Just slice a few into a salad – they taste really nice and nutty. Try the Marinated Mushrooms with Coriander recipe on p107. If you're a garlic lover try baking them with garlic butter (see p53). Try the tasty Mushroom Barlotto (p99). Try a simple Mushroom Omelette (p66). Try the flashy Open Lasagna with Porcini and Chestnut Mushrooms (p133). Any way – just try them.

ONIONS

Lots of people don't like raw onions. Plenty of people don't like them undercooked either. If you're one of them, try caramelising them by cooking them in a mixture of oil and butter over a moderate heat for about 15 minutes until they're soft and sweet (see p60). They also roast well (see 'carrots'). If you're adding them to a soup or something like a shepherd's pie, chop them up small and cook them well in oil or butter before you add the other ingredients. You won't notice they're there. Promise.

PARSNIPS

Parsnips, I admit, are a love/hate veg. If you're in the latter camp your best bet is to roast or grill them. They respond really well to a touch of sweetness. Try trickling a little honey over them. Also it helps if you prepare them properly.

Trim each parsnip at the top and bottom and peel. If they're large cut into quarters then cut away the central woody core.

PEPPERS

You probably dislike peppers one of two ways. Either you don't like them raw or you don't like them cooked. So try 'em the other way. If you hate raw peppers try roasting or grilling them (see Roast Mediterranean Vegetable Pasta Bake, p82, or GMVs, p52). If you don't like them cooked then try them raw with a dip (see p74) or briefly cooked in a stir-fry. Red and yellow peppers are sweeter and more digestible than green ones.

SPINACH

If you dislike the strong flavour of cooked spinach then try it raw as a salad. (You can buy ready-prepared salads which you can use straight out of the bag.) Add a few sliced raw mushrooms, a small handful of walnuts and the blue cheese dressing on p108 and you've got a really nice meal. Next step would be to sneak a few leaves into a curry or dal.

To prepare and cook spinach, tip the leaves into a sinkful of cold water and wash thoroughly. Pull off the stalks and central rib of any particularly large leaves. Drain off the water and press the spinach down into a large lidded saucepan. Place over a low heat and cook until the leaves start to collapse down. (You'll find they'll reduce to about a quarter of their original volume.) Turn them over and cook for a couple of minutes then drain thoroughly in a colander or sieve. Return to the pan with either a good chunk of butter or some oil, crushed garlic and a good pinch of garam masala. Treat frozen spinach the same way (i.e. no water, jazz it up once you've cooked it).

SPROUTS

I know sprout-haters hate sprouts with a vengeance but just try them once more for me. Don't cook them too long – 8-10 minutes is plenty. Cut across the base and remove the outer leaves. If the sprouts are particularly big cut a cross in the base to help them cook more quickly. Cover with boiling water, add salt and bring to the boil. Simmer until you can stick a sharp knife through them, then drain and put to one side. Heat a good lump of butter in the same pan, add a few flaked almonds and fry, shaking the pan till they begin to brown. Tip back the sprouts and toss with the almondy butter. Season with salt and pepper. Or slice and stir-fry them like cabbage.

SWEETCORN

Maybe it's the sweetness that puts you off. Try frozen rather than tinned sweetcorn, or try cutting it fresh off the cob. (Hold the cob upright on its base then cut down the sides of the cob to remove the kernels. Scrape the remains of the corn off with the tip of a teaspoon.) Avoid mixing corn with milk, cheese and other dairy products if you don't want it to taste too sweet. Try toasting the kernels in a dry pan and using them in a salad or a salsa.

Don't worry – I'm not going to suggest you spend all your spare time weeding and watering but if you've got a bit of space outside your student house you could easily grow a few herbs. Hardy, idiot-proof candidates are rosemary, thyme, mint, chives and sage, which will survive prolonged neglect once they are established. If you've got green fingers you could try parsley too.

Buy plants from garden centres or flower shops rather than attempt to transplant pot herbs you find in supermarkets which are less likely to survive out of doors.

SPROUTING SEEDS

If you can remember to tend them, you could try sprouting seeds which are fun to grow and highly nutritious. You can buy packs of mixed seeds from a health food shop or, more cheaply still, a pack of mung beans which you should be able to find in your local Asian grocer. You'll also need a couple of clean jam jars and either a J-Cloth (available from traditional hardware shops) or a piece of muslin and some rubber bands.

Rinse about $1^1/_2$ tbsp of seeds and put them in a jar. Pour some boiling water into a mug or jug and add cold water until you can comfortably dip your fingers in it. Pour it over the seeds, cover the jar with a piece of J-cloth or muslin, secure with a rubber band and leave overnight. Drain away the water then rinse the seeds twice a day with fresh lukewarm water, shaking the jar, then tipping it upside down and draining away the water so that the seeds don't rot. After 4 days you should be able to use them (in salads, sandwiches or stir-fries). They'll keep in the fridge for another 4 days. Start another batch of seeds so you have a constant supply.

KEEPING HERBS FRESH

Herbs generally keep best in a plastic bag in the salad drawer. The exception is coriander which is better stored in a tall glass (a beer glass is ideal) or jam jar full of water (particularly if you buy it loose from an ethnic grocer). Pull the plastic bag you bought it in over the top and secure it round the outside of the glass with a rubber band. Keep in the fridge and take it out and wash it as you need it, changing the water at least every other day. That way a big bunch should last you a week. Basil can also be temperamental and is best grown as a pot on the windowsill. If you do buy loose leaves wrap them in a damp kitchen towel then put them in a plastic bag in the salad drawer. Use them within a couple of days.

HOW NOT TO POISON YOUR FRIENDS

There are an awesome number of cases of food poisoning every year most of them perpetrated by dodgy restaurants and fast food traders but if you don't want to add to the statistics you do need to be at least vaguely aware of what constitutes food hygiene.

- Always wash your hands with soap thoroughly before starting to prepare food. Dry them with a hand towel or kitchen towel rather than your tea-towel.

- Keep your working surfaces clean. Or use a clean chopping board if they're not. Give them a good blitz every couple of days with an anti-bacterial cleaner.

- Keep the sink clean and free from teabags, potato peelings, leftover pasta and other grot.

- Wash your tea towels regularly and replace the washing up brush and/or scourers before they get too squalid.

- Keep the food you store in the fridge wrapped or covered – partly to avoid cross contamination, partly to stop them drying out.

- Don't refreeze frozen food that has thawed, especially ice cream.

- If you cook something to eat later or have perishable food left over, leave it to cool, then refrigerate it. (Never put warm food in the in the fridge) If you're going to eat it hot always reheat it thoroughly – that means simmer it for at least 5 minutes.

- Make sure your fridge is set at a cold enough setting for the amount of food it has in it. (Afraid there's no other way to check than buying a fridge thermometer.) Defrost and clean it thoroughly at least once a term.

- Refrigerate perishable food as soon as you can after buying it. Don't lug it round warm lecture rooms and coffee bars.

- Store the contents of half-finished tins like canned tomatoes or fruit in china, glass or plastic containers. Tins that are left open to the air can corrode.

- Get rid of anything that smells rank or shows obvious signs of decay – spots of mould, furry growths or generally unappealing squishy bits. Also potatoes that have sprouted or developed green patches. And anything that has passed its eat-by date. If in doubt chuck it out.

HOW LONG THINGS KEEP IN THE FRIDGE

It depends when and where you bought them and how quickly you put them away. Produce bought loose, especially from small shops, will generally need to be eaten sooner than pre-packed produce which has been chilled, though it also depends on the sell-by date. If you buy things cheap because they've reached or are nearing the end of their shelf life you should try to eat them the same day. Read the instructions on jars once you've opened them. Many products such as mayonnaise and cook-in sauces need to be kept in the fridge.

Within 24 hours
Pre-prepared salads, stir-fries and beansprouts.
Within 1-3 days
Mushrooms, soft fruit (e.g. strawberries), leftovers.
Within 4-6 days
Soft cheese, yoghurt, milk, tomatoes and other fresh veg and herbs.
A week to 10 days
Hard cheese, eggs.
A month or more
Butter and spreads (check the use-by date). Frozen foods (but ice cream should never be refrozen once thawed).

KEEP OUT OF THE FRIDGE

Garlic, onions and melons (will taint the other food you've got stored there, especially butter). Bananas and avocadoes go black and soggy. Potatoes are best stored in a paper bag. If not, tear open the plastic bag so the air can get to them.

...OR SCALD, ELECTROCUTE, OR SET FIRE TO THEM

More fires start in the kitchen than in any other room in the house – usually when someone just wanders off and forgets they've left something on the hob. Apart from that...

 DON'T buy dodgy second hand appliances with frayed cords

 DON'T leave kitchen towel, tea towels or oven gloves near the hob where they can catch fire

 DON'T cook with floppy sleeves
DON'T cook when you're legless
DON'T leave pan handles sticking out from the stove

 DON'T leave the hob, oven or appliances like sandwich toasters on when you've finished cooking

 DON'T use a metal or foil container in a microwave

 DON'T let electrical leads dangle into water
DON'T leave your toaster full of crumbs and your grill pan clogged with fat. It's asking for a flare up.

WHAT TO DO IF THE OIL IN A PAN CATCHES FIRE

Throw a damp towel over it to exclude the air. (Wring it out under the tap.) Never throw water on an oil fire. If it's out of control get everyone out of the kitchen, shut the door and call 999.

IT'S BLINDINGLY OBVIOUS, BUT...

 Read any new recipe through in full before you start cooking. Laying out and preparing the ingredients you need also helps.

 If you're buyinig pre-packed foods make sure you read the instructions.

 Most recipes in this book can be halved or doubled but spices and seasonings don't usually need to be changed that much. Use a little bit less or a little bit more, tasting as you go.

 Ovens – particularly student ovens – are temperamental and can be slightly hotter or cooler than the norm. (In a gas oven the top of the oven is always hotter than the bottom.) If you find your food is generally overcooked use a setting lower than I recommend. If it's undercooked turn it up a setting. Don't keep opening the oven door while food is cooking.

 Always preheat the oven before you put the food in.

 Remember what time you put the food on to cook. (A timer helps.)

 Don't use the same cooking fat continuously – it will taste rank. And don't pour fat down the sink – it'll block it. Cool it then pour it into a disposable container like a yoghurt pot and put it in the bin.

 Plates and pans are easier to wash when you've finished using them rather than three days later. If you have got to that stage soak them first.

 It's much easier (and more hygienic) to wash up in hot water than lukewarm or cold.

 If you use a metal spoon, scourer or brillo pad on a non-stick pan you'll ruin it.

A WORD ABOUT MEASUREMENTS...

Some of the best cooks cook without measuring anything so why bother with measurements? Because while chefs are used to measuring things by eye, feel and taste, you are more likely to succeed if you know roughly how much of what to put in. That said, you don't have to take what I say as gospel. If I recommend using 400g of onions and you only have 350g that's not going to make a big difference. But doubling the quantity of a strongly flavoured spice like chilli powder is.

SPOON SIZES

If you don't have a set of measuring spoons (or have lost them) you can use ordinary ones. A teaspoon is the size of spoon you use for stirring tea or coffee or eating yoghurt out of a pot. A dessertspoon is the type you use to eat cereal or soup, while a tablespoon is the size of spoon you would use for serving food. Put another way a teaspoon contains 5ml, a dessertspoon 10ml and a tablespoon 15ml.

Spoons can be described in a recipe as level, rounded or heaped. This is because some ingredients like honey or chopped herbs aren't easy to measure out precisely. Level is where the contents of the spoon are literally level with the edge of the bowl of the spoon. Rounded is where they are slightly domed, and heaped is where they're piled on the spoon. (You need to use a bit of common sense about this. You could for example get an absolutely massive tablespoon of, say, mashed potato which would be equivalent to about 3 or 4 ordinary tablespoons.) Some recipes also call for $1/2$ or $1/4$ teaspoons – usually for powerful ingredients like spices. A pinch is the amount you can hold between your thumb and forefinger and a handful is exactly that – the amount you can pick up and hold in your hand (without trying overhard to cram it in).

An ordinary mug is a reasonably good measure for liquid. If you fill it up to the level you'd normally fill it for a coffee it'll hold about 225ml (i.e. 8 fl oz). So far as cooking terms are concerned I've tried to keep it simple but if a phrase has slipped in you don't understand or if something goes horribly wrong email me at **fiona@beyondbakedbeans.com**.

...AND TIMINGS

You'll see that many of the ingredients listed in the recipes are pre-prepared. That's partly to avoid repetition, partly to get over the idea that it helps to get everything you need ready before you start cooking. So you may find to begin with that recipes take slightly longer than I've indicated. Once you've made a recipe once or twice you'll find it much easier and quicker to make it.

Recipes that are suitable for vegans are marked with this symbol.

SOLO

When you first get to uni, chances are you'll be living in hall and sharing a kitchen with 8 or 10 other students. Not the easiest environment to start your cooking career, particularly if you're veggie and they're not. So, this section is based on the assumption that you're mainly going to be cooking for one or, if you find a couple of like-minded individuals on your floor, for two or three. And you won't have much in the way of equipment and that you may not have a conventional oven.

I also realise you may have things on your mind other than food and that for most of you it's going to be more of a question of keeping body and soul together than toiling over the cooker creating a slap-up feast. So these recipes are quick, simple and most can be cooked in one pan. Oh, and I forgot to say, they're cheap and delicious too!

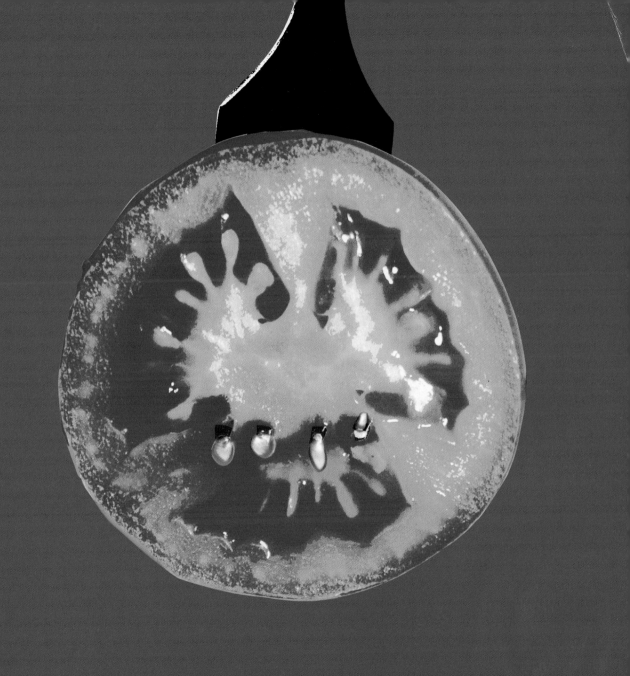

If you're cooking for one, tinned beans are one of the most useful and flexible staples you can have in your storecupboard. With a couple of other ingredients you can whizz up a meal in less than 15 minutes – real fast food.

BASQUE BUTTERBEAN STEW

Serves 1-2 Ve
UNDER 15 MINUTES

This simple combination of onions, peppers and smoked pepper is typical of the Basque regions of Northern Spain and France.

2 tbsp light olive oil or sunflower oil
1 small to medium onion, peeled and thinly sliced
125g frozen peppers or a small red pepper, deseeded and cut into strips
1 clove of garlic, peeled and crushed
$1/2$ tsp paprika (preferably Spanish pimenton)
A small (200g) tin of tomatoes or $1/2$ a 400g tin
1 400g tin of butter beans or chickpeas drained and rinsed
Salt and freshly ground black pepper
A heaped tbsp chopped fresh parsley (optional)

Put a large frying pan or wok over a medium heat, add the oil, heat for 30 seconds then add the onion. Fry for 2-3 minutes until beginning to soften then add the peppers, garlic and paprika. Continue to stir-fry for another couple of minutes then add the tomatoes and their juice, breaking them up with a wooden spoon or spatula. Cook the vegetables for another 2 minutes then add the drained butterbeans and cook for another 3-4 minutes until heated through. Season to taste with salt and pepper, stir in the parsley if you have some, then serve in a large soup bowl (or bowls).

• Without the beans this also makes a great sauce for pasta or a topping for a baked potato. You could also serve the sauce with a couple of fried eggs.

LEEK AND LEMON BEANS

Serves 2 Ve
UNDER 15 MINUTES

This is one of those neat little recipes that came about by accident when I was rooting around for something to eat. Warm, it makes a tasty accompaniment for veggie sausages. Cold, a lovely fresh-tasting salad.

2 small to medium leeks or one large leek
2 tbsp olive oil plus a little extra if needed
1 400g tin flageolet or cannellini beans
2-3 tsp of fresh lemon juice
1 heaped tbsp finely chopped parsley
1/2 tsp chopped fresh thyme or 1/4 tsp dried thyme
  (optional)
Freshly ground black pepper

Clean and slice the leeks as described on p58. Heat the oil in a small pan and stir-fry the leeks for 2-3 minutes until beginning to soften. Add the beans, 2 tsp of lemon juice and herbs, stir, cover the pan and cook over a low to medium heat for another 3-4 minutes until the beans and leeks are soft. Season with black pepper and extra lemon juice and oil to taste.

- If you share a house with a garden or patio grow some thyme. It comes in handy for all sorts of dishes (see Grow Your Own p28).

BAKED BEANS WITH SPRING ONION SABJI

Serves 2 Ve
UNDER 15 MINUTES

Just to prove I've got nothing against baked beans here's a recipe I've adapted from Vicky Bhogal's fabulous Cooking Like Mummyji, *a book you'll love if you're into spicy food. Sabji by the way means a vegetarian dish.*

1 tbsp oil
1 medium onion, peeled and chopped finely
1 garlic clove, peeled and crushed
1/2 tsp ground turmeric
1/2 tsp garam masala
A pinch of chilli powder or a few drops of hot
  pepper sauce
1 green chilli, de-seeded and finely chopped
2-3 spring onions, trimmed and diagonally sliced
400g can of baked beans
2 heaped tbsp chopped fresh coriander
Salt and lemon juice to taste

Heat the oil, add the onion and fry till soft. Add the garlic, spices, chilli and spring onions and stir-fry for a couple of minutes. Tip in the baked beans and coriander, stir well and heat through. Season to taste with salt (about 1/4 tsp) and lemon juice (a good squeeze). You can simply serve this on toast as usual but it's also good with pitta bread or rice and onion raita or a dollop of yoghurt.

MOROCCAN-SPICED CHICKPEAS WITH SPINACH

Serves 1-2 Ve
UNDER 15 MINUTES

This Moroccan spicing is one of my favourites – worth making in a big batch so you just have it to hand when you need it. Note the sneaky inclusion of fresh greens which together with the tomatoes really makes this quite a healthy dish.

2 tbsp light olive or vegetable oil
1 medium onion (about 110g), peeled and roughly chopped
2 cloves of garlic, peeled and crushed
2 rounded tsp Moroccan spice mix (see p12) or 1 tsp each of ground coriander and cumin, 1/2 tsp turmeric and 1/4 tsp chilli powder
1 200g can or 1/2 a 400g can of tomatoes
1 400g can of chickpeas, drained and rinsed
A handful of roughly chopped fresh spinach or cabbage leaves and/or 1 heaped tbsp chopped fresh coriander leaves
Salt
A small carton of natural, unsweetened yoghurt or soy yoghurt (optional)

Heat the oil in a frying pan and fry the onion for about 4-5 minutes until soft. Stir in the garlic and spice mix and fry for a few seconds then tip in the tomatoes and break them up with a wooden spoon, spatula or fork. Bring to the boil, add the drained, rinsed chickpeas, cover the pan and simmer for 7-8 minutes. Chuck in the spinach or cabbage leaves and coriander (if using) and cook for another 2 minutes. Add salt to taste. You could serve this with a dollop of yoghurt and some pitta bread or naan.

• This also tastes great cold. Mash any leftover chickpeas and use them to fill a pitta bread.

ITALIAN BEAN AND PASTA SOUP

Serves 2-3 Ve
15-30 MINUTES

Actually this is more like a substantial bean stew. Also a good dish to make for large numbers – it's easy enough to double up the quantities.

4-5 tbsp olive oil
1 medium onion (about 110g), peeled and roughly chopped
1-2 cloves of garlic
1 medium to large tinned or fresh tomato, skinned (see p41) and finely chopped
400g tin of borlotti or cannellini beans
600ml hot vegetable stock made from 2 heaped tsp of vegetable bouillon powder or a vegetable stock cube
A handful of pasta shapes (about 55g)
100g frozen cut green beans or finely shredded fresh cabbage

Salt and freshly ground black pepper
2 heaped tbsp chopped parsley (optional but good)

Heat 2 tbsp of the oil in a large saucepan or casserole dish and cook the onion for about 4-5 minutes until soft. Stir in the garlic and tomato, cook for a minute then add the borlotti beans and stock. Bring to the boil, chuck in the pasta and frozen beans or cabbage, bring back to the boil and cook for about 10 minutes or until the pasta is soft. Season to taste with salt and pepper, stir in the parsley (if using) and ladle into warm bowls. Trickle a little extra olive oil over each portion before serving.

- To make this more like a conventional minestrone add an extra tomato and some juice from the can and sprinkle with Parmesan rather than olive oil.
- Stir a heaped tsp of pesto into any leftovers for a richer flavour.

BLACK EYE BEAN SALSA Serves 1-2

 UNDER 15 MINUTES

You could call this a salad but somehow it sounds more sexy as a salsa. Either way it's a great accompaniment for veggie burgers or felafel. You can obviously vary the veg depending on what you have available. Chopped celery or sweetcorn would be fine.

A small (300g) can of black eye beans
  or ²/₃ a 400g tin of red kidney beans
¹/₂ a small onion, peeled and finely chopped
8-10 cherry tomatoes, quartered
¹/₄ of a cucumber, de-seeded and cut into small cubes
¹/₂ a small red pepper, de-seeded and diced
1 tbsp fresh lemon juice plus extra to taste if needed
4 tbsp olive oil
2 heaped tbsp chopped fresh coriander or parsley
Salt and a little hot pepper sauce, cayenne pepper or chilli powder

Drain the beans, put them in a colander or sieve, rinse them and shake them dry. Put them in a bowl with the chopped onion, tomatoes, cucumber and pepper. Spoon over the lemon, olive oil and herbs and season with salt and a few shakes of hot pepper sauce or a little chilli powder. Mix well, taste and adjust the seasoning if necessary.

Other recipes based on a tin...
Stuffed Pitta Pockets with Mexican Beans (see p61), Gently Spiced Lentils with Tomatoes, and Carrot and Lentil Pilau (for both, see p96), and Mixed Bean and Crumbly White Cheese Salad (see p55).

Given that pasta is the ultimate student staple you're going to be eating a lot of pasta meals. But they don't all have to taste the same. You may, of course, want to take advantage of the huge array of pasta sauces that are available but you can make your own at a fraction of the price. They'll taste better too.

How to cook pasta
For one helping you'll need 100g-125g of dried pasta depending how hungry you are (Italian brands are best, don't bother with fresh). Boil a full kettle and tip the water into a large pan. Bring back to the boil, add the pasta and about 1/2 tsp salt, stir, then cook for the time recommended on the pack. To check if the pasta is done, hook a strand or piece out of the pan and bite into it. It should be neither hard nor soft and soggy. Drain it in a colander or sieve, saving a little of the cooking water to add to your sauce. Return the pasta to the pan then toss with enough sauce just to coat it lightly. Don't drown it.

• The most common mistake people make is not using enough water. You need a litre for every 100g of pasta you cook.

STRIPPED-DOWN TOMATO SAUCE

Serves 2, generously or 1 person, twice
UNDER 15 MINUTES

Once you've made this – which needn't cost you more than 50p – you'll wonder why anyone uses a ready-made tomato sauce. It makes enough for two meals which you can vary with other ingredients (see below). Incidentally don't bother with tomatoes that are flavoured with herbs and garlic. Just simple whole tomatoes will do.

2 tbsp olive oil
1 clove of garlic, peeled and crushed
1 400g tin of tomatoes in their own juice
Salt, pepper and sugar to taste
2 tbsp chopped fresh parsley (optional)

Heat the oil in a large frying pan. Add the garlic. Tip in the tin of tomatoes and crush with a fork or a wooden spoon. Season with salt, pepper and a pinch of sugar and simmer for about 10 minutes till thick and jammy. That's it, basically. I would add a couple of spoonfuls of chopped fresh parsley and some freshly grated Parmesan or Grana Padano to serve but grated Cheddar will do fine.

You can also add
• 1/2 tsp dried oregano or herbes de Provence.
• A few chopped pitted black or green olives and/ or 1 tbsp of capers rinsed and roughly chopped.

- A chopped red pepper fried in a little olive oil and a little chilli sauce.
- A small aubergine or 2 medium sized courgettes, cubed and shallow fried.
- Some Quorn or Vegemince for a spag bol.

SUMMER SPAGHETTI WITH CHERRY TOMATOES AND GOATS' CHEESE

Serves 1 **UNDER 15 MINUTES**

This is a pared down version of a lovely recipe from TV chef Gennaro Contaldo, Jamie Oliver's great Italian friend and mentor. You can cut the cost even further by substituting a crumbly white cheese like Cheshire for the goats' cheese and parsley for fresh basil but this version is particularly delicious.

About 200g cherry tomatoes or 2 medium to large ripe tomatoes
2 tbsp olive oil (the best you can afford)
1 clove of garlic, peeled and finely chopped (optional)
8-10 large, fresh basil leaves or 2 tbsp finely chopped parsley
100-125g dried spaghetti or linguine
50g goats' cheese or other mild white cheese such as Cheshire or Wensleydale
Salt, freshly ground black pepper, sugar and vinegar to taste

De-stalk and roughly chop the tomatoes (see footnote). Put them in a bowl with the olive oil (and chopped garlic, if using). Tear the basil leaves into small pieces and add them too. Season the tomatoes with salt, pepper and a few drops of vinegar plus a little sugar if they're not quite ripe enough and mix together well. Cook the pasta in boiling water for the time recommended on the pack (see 'How to cook pasta', opposite). Drain and return to the pan then tip over the sauce. Mix well together and leave for a minute while you crumble the goats' cheese. Tip the pasta onto a large plate or bowl and scatter the cheese on top.

- If you're using normal-sized tomatoes you can peel them first by making a small nick in the skin, and plunging them into a bowl full of boiling water. Leave them for a minute then drain and rinse them under cold water. The skins should come off easily.
- You could add a handful of cooked broad beans to the sauce to make it more substantial.

Mushrooms are one of my favourite ingredients because of their intense, savoury, meaty flavour. The only downside is that they can turn any light coloured sauce a dirty grey. Dark open portabella mushrooms are the worst culprits in this respect, but then they have more flavour. The trick is to cook the mushrooms beforehand until any liquid evaporates.

MUSHROOM AND EGG PASTA 1 (AKA MUSHROOM CARBONARA)

Serves 1 UNDER 15 MINUTES

Basically a spaghetti carbonara with mushrooms rather than bacon. But none the worse for that.

2 tbsp cooking oil
125g dried spaghetti
1 small or 1/2 a medium onion, peeled and finely
   chopped
1 small clove of garlic, peeled and crushed
About 125g button mushrooms, cleaned
   (see footnote) and sliced
2 medium eggs
2 tbsp freshly grated Parmesan or Grana Padano
   plus extra for serving
Freshly ground black pepper and a little salt

Heat the oil in a frying pan over a medium heat, add the onion and cook gently for 5 minutes or until soft. Stir in the garlic then turn up the heat, add the mushrooms and fry for about 3-4 minutes until any liquid has evaporated. Leave the pan over a low heat while you cook the spaghetti for the time recommended on the pack (see 'How to cook pasta', p40). While it's cooking beat the eggs with 2 tbsp of the Parmesan and season with freshly ground black pepper and a little salt. When the pasta is cooked, drain it thoroughly and return it to the pan off the heat. Quickly tip in the beaten eggs and mix thoroughly so the egg 'cooks' in the hot pasta. Then lightly mix in the mushrooms, season again with black pepper and serve with extra Parmesan.

- The easiest way to clean mushrooms is to gently rub any dirt or grit off under cold running water. Don't leave them soaking in water.
- You could also add a few thawed frozen peas.

MUSHROOM AND EGG PASTA 2

Serves 1 UNDER 15 MINUTES

This time the egg isn't in the sauce a la carbonara but in the pasta – there's a real affinity between authentic Italian egg pasta and mushrooms.

1 tbsp of olive oil
A good slice of butter (about 20g)
125g-150g 'open' or portabella mushrooms,
   wiped and thinly sliced or any other flavourful
   mushrooms
1 clove of garlic, peeled and crushed
A pinch of salt and pepper

125g dried egg tagliatelle or fettucine
2 tbsp double cream (optional)
$1/4$ tsp paprika
Lemon juice to taste
1 heaped tbsp finely chopped parsley

Heat the oil in a large frying pan, add $2/3$ of the butter and when it starts foaming chuck in the mushrooms and stir them round. Add the garlic, season with salt and pepper and a pinch (about $1/4$ tsp) of paprika, stir and fry for a 3-4 minutes until any liquid has evaporated. Leave the mushrooms on a low heat while you put the pasta on to cook, following the instructions on the pack (see 'How to cook pasta', p40). It'll probably take about 3-4 minutes. Take a couple of tablespoons of the pasta water and add it to the mushrooms then drain the pasta and return it to the pan, stirring in the remaining butter. Stir the cream into the mushrooms (if using) and check the seasoning, adding a squeeze of lemon juice and more salt and pepper if you think it needs it. Then stir in the chopped parsley. Serve the buttered pasta with the mushroom sauce over the top.

- This sauce also makes a good topping for hot buttered toast.

QUICK BUTTERED VEGETABLE PASTA Serves 1
UNDER 15 MINUTES

Frozen mixed veg are an easy and cheap way of getting your 5-a-day.

125g pasta shapes
A good slice of butter (about 25g)
150g frozen mixed vegetables
A good squeeze of fresh lemon juice or 1 tbsp Jif or equivalent squirty lemon
1 heaped tbsp finely chopped chives or parsley (optional, but good)
Salt and pepper

Pour a kettleful of boiling water into a pan, bring back to the boil, add salt and tip in the pasta. Cook for the time recommended on the packet. Meanwhile melt the butter in another small pan, add 1 tbsp of water and tip in the frozen veg. Cover with a lid or plate, bring to the boil and simmer for 3 to 4 minutes. Once the pasta is cooked, drain it thoroughly and return it to the pan. Pour over the buttered veg, season to taste with salt, pepper and lemon juice and add the chopped herbs (if using).

- You could add some grated Parmesan but it doesn't really need it. A couple of tablespoons of double cream, though, at the end, would be fab.

If you like your pasta to pack a bit of a punch these recipes are for you. Don't be alarmed by the amount of garlic in some of them. Once garlic is cooked it's much milder and sweeter in flavour.

BROCCOLI, CHILLI AND GARLIC PASTA

Serves 2 Ve
15-30 MINUTES

This spicy recipe is based on the classic Italian recipe – spaghetti con aglio, olio e peperoncini (spaghetti with garlic, oil and hot pepper) but it's a good way to sneak in those good-for-you greens without too much pain.

Half a head (4-5 large cloves) of garlic, peeled
4 tbsp olive oil
$1/2$-1 tsp dried crushed chillies or $1/2$-1 tsp hot chilli sauce
1 head of broccoli or a small pack of broccoli florets
250g wholewheat or ordinary spaghetti or pasta shapes
Salt

Slice the garlic thinly then put it in a small saucepan with the oil and the crushed chillies. Place over a ring or gas burner and cook on the lowest possible heat for about 15 minutes until the garlic is soft and transparent. Meanwhile cut the broccoli up into very small florets and microwave, steam or cook for 3 minutes in boiling water until just tender. Drain thoroughly. Cook the pasta following the instructions on the pack and reserve a little of the cooking water. Drain, tip in the broccoli and garlicky oil, season with salt and chilli sauce if you haven't already added chilli and toss together. Pour in a little of the pasta cooking water (about 2 tbsp) and place back on the hob for a minute or two to warm through, then serve.

GUTSY GARLIC AND OLIVE PASTA

Serves 1 Ve
UNDER 15 MINUTES

This is not a pasta dish for the faint-hearted. Don't even attempt it if you don't like olives. Or garlic, for that matter.

125g wholewheat pasta
$2^1/2$ tbsp olive oil
175g ripe cherry tomatoes, halved or $1/2$ a 400g tin of cherry tomatoes
Salt, freshly ground black pepper and a little sugar
2 large cloves of garlic, peeled and crushed
75g pitted black olives
$1/2$ level tsp oregano or herbes de Provence
1 heaped tbsp fresh parsley (optional but good)

Cook the pasta, as described on p40, following the timing recommended on the pack. While the pasta is cooking heat 1 tbsp of the oil in a frying pan, add the tomatoes, season with salt, pepper and a little sugar and fry over a medium heat until beginning to blacken. Turn the heat down and add another tablespoon of oil, the garlic, olives and oregano, stir and cook for a minute then add 3 tbsp of the cooking water from the pasta. Simmer for about 3 minutes then turn off the heat and stir in the parsley. Drain the pasta, toss it with the remaining olive oil then tip it onto a plate or shallow bowl and top with the pasta sauce.

ALL SEASONS PASTA SALAD

Serves 2 or 1 twice Ve
15-30 MINUTES

'All seasons' because it relies on ingredients you can buy year round. This is an infinitely adaptable salad that you can fiddle around with depending on your mood and what you've got to hand.
If you haven't got any leftover pasta just cook some from scratch and rinse it with cold water.

2 tbsp olive oil
1 small onion, peeled and finely sliced or ½ a bunch of spring onions, trimmed and diagonally sliced
125g frozen peppers or a medium red pepper, quartered and sliced
3-4 sundried tomato halves (soaked in warm water if not preserved in oil)
1-2 cloves of garlic, peeled and crushed
2 tbsp passata, creamed tomatoes or juice from a can of tomatoes
300g cooked pasta (about 150g dried pasta)
1-2 tsp wine vinegar or a good squeeze of lemon juice
2 heaped tbsp chopped parsley – or, even better, a handful of torn basil leaves
Salt and pepper

Heat a frying pan and add the oil. Heat for a minute then add the sliced onion and peppers and stir-fry till soft (about 4-5 minutes for frozen peppers, a little longer for fresh ones). Slice the sundried tomatoes and add to the pan with the garlic. Stir well and cook for a minute then add the passata. Tip in the cooked pasta, mix well and season to taste with salt, pepper and wine vinegar or lemon juice. Stir in the parsley or basil and leave to cool for 10-15 minutes (or eat straight away – no reason why not). Save half for a meal the next day.

Some good additions
- A few slices of Mozzarella or some crumbled goats' cheese, Feta or other white cheese.
- Some other preserved Italian vegetables like artichokes or aubergines (you can buy these loose in an Italian deli).
- A few capers and/or olives rinsed and roughly chopped.
- ½ tsp of chilli flakes (added when you fry the onions and peppers) or a ¼ tsp chilli powder.

Although stir-fries and noodles would probably rank second to pasta, with most students they're an even quicker way of feeding yourself. Again, you don't need expensive stir-fry sauces which are often full of additives, but cheap packets of stir-fry veg do save a lot of work.

- Supermarkets sell cheap packets of stir-fry for about 80p. The only downside is they don't keep that long. Try and buy one with a couple of days still to go before the 'sell-by' date runs out and use it as soon as possible. With the other half of the pack you could make a Quick Spicy Beansprout Salad (see p56).

SIMPLE STIR-FRY WITH CASHEW NUTS

Serves 1 Ve
UNDER 15 MINUTES

About the easiest meal you can make.
Cheap too if you buy broken rather than whole nuts.

3 tbsp cooking oil
50g cashew nuts
2 cloves of garlic, peeled
1/2 a 300g bag of beansprout stir-fry (see footnote)
2 tbsp light soy sauce

Heat the oil over a medium heat in a wok or large frying pan. Chuck in the cashew nuts and garlic and stir-fry for a about a minute till they are lightly browned. Remove from the pan with a slotted spoon or fish slice and discard the garlic. Turn up the heat then add the veg. Stir-fry for a minute then add a splash of water (about 2 tbsp) and the soy sauce. Cook for a few seconds more then serve topped with the crispy nuts.

CHINESE CUCUMBER STIR-FRY

Serves 2 Ve
UNDER 15 MINUTES

I was given this recipe by one of the regular student visitors to my website, Louisa-Jane Evans, who in turn got it from her mother who is Malaysian-Chinese. The original has chicken in it but I think it works equally well without. Either way it's blissfully simple comfort food, the kind to eat when you're feeling poorly or have a hell of a hangover. Or both.

1 cucumber
2 tbsp sunflower or peanut oil
3-4 thin slices of ginger
2 medium cloves of garlic
Half a cup (100ml) vegetable stock made with
    3/4 tsp vegetable bouillon powder or 1/3 of an
    organic vegetable stock cube
1 tsp cornflour mixed with a little warm boiled
    water
1/2 tsp granulated sugar

Peel the cucumber thinly (a vegetable peeler is easiest for this). Slice an end off the peeled cucumber and hold pointing away from you. Slice your first piece off at an angle from the end so that you get a piece that looks a bit like a tangerine segment. Rotate the cucumber a little, and repeat. It's important to cut the cucumber correctly, including a bit of the core in each segment so that it all cooks at the same speed. Heat a wok or large pan, heat the oil and fry the ginger, adding the garlic when you can smell the aroma of the cooked ginger. Next add the cucumber. Stir-fry for about a minute on a high heat. Turn the heat down, add the stock and the cornflour mixture and a little sugar and put a lid on the pan or wok to simmer for about 4-5 minutes. Serve with fluffy rice (see p50).

CRISPY TOFU, SESAME AND BEANSPROUT STIR-FRY

Serves 1-2 Ⓥ
UNDER 15 MINUTES (PLUS MARINADING TIME)

If you shudder at the thought of tofu, try this delicious way of cooking it. The initial marinating takes time, so find something else to do in between.

75g-100g firm tofu
2½ tbsp sunflower or vegetable oil
2 tbsp soy sauce
1-2 cloves of garlic, very finely sliced
A little flour for coating the tofu
A small pack or ½ a medium sized pack beansprout stir-fry
2 spring onions, trimmed and finely sliced (optional)
1 rounded tsp toasted sesame seeds (see footnote)
A little hot chilli sauce (optional)

Cut the tofu into four even sized cubes, pop them in a plastic bag and pour over 1 tbsp each of the oil and the soy sauce. Add one of the sliced garlic cloves, seal the bag and shake gently to ensure all the tofu is coated. Marinate for an hour then pat dry, and dip in the flour. Heat the remaining oil in a frying pan or wok and fry the tofu pieces for a couple of minutes each side until brown and crispy. Remove the tofu from the pan and lay it on a piece of kitchen towel. Turn up the heat, tip the beansprouts, veg and the extra garlic (and onions, if using) into the pan and fry for a minute or two then add the remaining soy sauce and fry for another minute. Serve topped with the tofu and scatter with sesame seeds. Serve with extra soy and chilli sauce to taste.

- Toast sesame seeds by frying them in a dry pan (i.e. without any oil) over a moderate heat for a few minutes, shaking the pan occasionally. Turn off the heat and continue to shake the seeds occasionally for a couple of minutes as they cool.
- Instead of the sesame seeds you could top with a crumbled sheet of toasted nori seaweed (see p49).

Even quicker to prepare than pasta, all you need to do with most noodles is soak them and add them to a stir-fry or a soup. The most common kind you're likely to find (apart from the ubiquitous Pot Noodle) are egg noodles (virtually interchangeable with pasta and best for stir-fries) and rice noodles which are good for Thai-style stir-fries and soups. But I also really like soba noodles which have much more taste and texture – more like a wholewheat pasta. You can use them in stir-fries but also cold in salads. I'm not being sniffy about instant noodles (except Pot Noodles, which are gross). There are times (before dashing out in the evening or in the middle of revising) when they're the easiest way to fill the gap in your stomach. The best flavoured ones tend to come from Japan; the cheapest from specialist Chinese or other Asian supermarkets, but be wary as many of them are stuffed with additives including monosodium glutamate.

ALMOST INSTANT NOODLES

Serves 1 Ve
UNDER 15 MINUTES

If you've time (like about 2 minutes) and the ingredients handy this will improve almost any pack of noodles.

1 packet instant Japanese soba noodles with
    sauce

Any of the following
- A little freshly grated ginger and/or garlic or half a teaspoon of ginger and/or garlic paste.
- A good squeeze of lemon or lime.
- Some chopped fresh coriander leaves.
- Some sweet chilli sauce.

Make up the noodles according to the instructions on the packet. Once hot, stir in as many of the other ingredients as you fancy.

GLISTENING GREENS WITH SOBA NOODLES

Serves 1 Ve
UNDER 15 MINUTES

Stir-frying is a really quick, healthy way of serving veg without losing valuable nutrients in the cooking water. It works particularly well with dark, strong-flavoured greens like savoy cabbage, spring greens and kale.

100g soba noodles or wholewheat spaghetti
1/4 of a small dark green cabbage or a head of
    spring greens or a good handful of kale,
    preferably organic
2 tbsp cooking oil
1-2 tbsp light soy sauce

Soak the soba noodles following the instructions on the pack or cook the spaghetti, drain, and rinse with cold water. Remove any tough or damaged outer leaves from the cabbage and cut away the tough central white core. Finely slice the rest of the leaves and rinse under cold water. Heat the wok until very hot then add the oil. Tip in the greens and stir-fry them for a couple of minutes, turning them with a couple of wooden spoons or some kitchen tongs. Add the soy sauce and a splash of water and cook, stirring, for another minute. Add the noodles to the pan, toss together and serve.

- You can crank up the seasoning on this by adding some crushed garlic or grated ginger to the greens as you stir-fry them, and/or adding a few drops of sesame oil at the end, but it's pretty good as it is.

MUSHROOM AND NORI NOODLES

Serves 2 Ve
UNDER 15 MINUTES

This recipe may looks as if it contains a dauntingly large number of strange – and expensive – ingredients but they're mostly ones you can use for several recipes. And if you're into these fabulously savoury Japanese flavours they're ones you'll always want to have to hand. Nori is the addictive element – it's the seaweed that's used to wrap sushi rolls.

2 tbsp sunflower, rapeseed or vegetable oil
1 tsp sesame oil plus extra for seasoning or 1 tbsp toasted sesame seeds (see p47)
1/2 a bunch of spring onions (about 4-5), trimmed and finely sliced
100g shitake or chestnut mushrooms, rinsed and finely sliced
1 clove of garlic, peeled and crushed
250ml stock made with 1 rounded tsp of brown miso or a sachet of instant miso soup
1 tbsp soy sauce plus extra to taste if you think it needs it
300g soaked or ready to cook medium wheat noodles (e.g. Amoy Straight to Wok)
2 toasted nori seaweed sheets*

Heat a wok or large frying pan for a couple of minutes. Add the two oils then tip in the spring onions and shitake mushrooms and stir-fry for a couple of minutes. Add the garlic, stir, then pour in the stock and soy sauce. Bring to the boil and cook for a minute then chuck in the noodles. Pull them apart gently as they heat through till all the strands are separate and thoroughly coated with the sauce. Adjust the seasoning, adding extra soy sauce and sesame oil if you think it needs it. Turn off the heat and scrunch up the toasted nori in your hand. Drop it into the noodles, toss well and serve in warm bowls.

- To toast nori hold each sheet above a gas burner with a pair of kitchen tongs so that it crisps up but doesn't burn.

Good rice is one of life's luxuries. I know brown rice is better for you but I simply can't resist the taste of white basmati. It has a purity and delicacy that brown rice lacks and is quicker to cook. Look out for broken basmati which is about a third cheaper.

PERFECT FLUFFY RICE

Serves 2

This is the kind of rice that goes perfectly with a curry. The key is to cook it in lots of water, like pasta.

125g basmati rice
1/2 tsp salt

If you've bought very cheap rice put it in a sieve and wash it under cold water, picking out any stones or pieces of grit (not necessary with big brands like Tilda). Boil a kettle full of water, pour it into a saucepan, bring back to the boil, salt the water and tip in the rice. Give it a stir then boil for 10 minutes. Drain the rice in a colander or sieve then balance the sieve over the saucepan and cover it with a piece of kitchen towel. After 5 minutes, pour away any water that has accumulated in the pan, tip in the rice and fork it through to fluff it up. If you want to set some aside to make a rice salad add the dressing while it's still warm (see Tomato, Herb and Rice Salad, opposite).

PILAU RICE

Serves 2 Ve 15-30 MINUTES

Great with dry curries or simply to eat on its own.

1 tbsp sunflower oil
1 small onion or half a medium onion, peeled and finely chopped
A teaspoon of whole masala spices, roughly crushed (see footnote) or pilau rice seasoning
125 ml basmati rice (measured in a jug) rinsed and drained
50g frozen peas (optional)
1/4 tsp salt

Heat the oil in a lidded saucepan. Cook the onion uncovered over a medium heat for 8-10 minutes stirring occasionally (you want to brown it rather than sweat it). Add the whole spices or pilau rice seasoning, stir and cook for a minute. Then add the rice, stir and cook for a further minute. Add 250ml of boiling water, salt and the frozen peas (if using), stir, cover and cook for 10-12 minutes until the water is absorbed. Turn off the heat and leave for a further 5 minutes. Fluff up the rice with a fork, fishing out any tough bits of husk and serve.

• Use a pestle and mortar to crush the spices, or the end of a rolling pin or the side of a can.

Leftover rice

This is better used sooner rather than later. Don't keep it for more than 48 hours, even under ideal conditions (well covered in the fridge). For the egg-fried rice you want it chilled when you start. For the salad, rather contrarily, you want it warm.

EGG-FRIED RICE Serves 2

UNDER 15 MINUTES

A comforting dish which I'd be happy to eat at least once a week.

3 medium or 2 large fresh eggs, preferably free-range
2 tbsp sunflower or vegetable oil
1/2 bunch of spring onions, trimmed and finely sliced or 1 small onion peeled and finely chopped
About 275g chilled cooked basmati rice (125g of uncooked rice)
100g frozen peas, cooked or thawed
1-11/2 tbsp light soy sauce

Break the eggs into a bowl and beat them lightly. Heat a wok or large frying pan over a moderate heat and pour in the oil. Tip in the onions and stir-fry for 2 minutes until beginning to soften. Add the eggs and stir until almost all the liquid egg has disappeared. Add the rice and peas and stir-fry for a couple of minutes until hot through. Add soy sauce to taste.

• To make this more filling you could add sliced button mushrooms.

TOMATO, HERB AND RICE SALAD

Serves 2 **V** **UNDER 15 MINUTES (ONCE RICE IS COOKED)**

This fresh, summer salad is best made – like most rice salads – with freshly cooked warm (not hot) rice.

About 225g freshly cooked rice (100g uncooked)
1 tbsp light olive oil
A few drops of balsamic vinegar or seasoned rice vinegar or wine vinegar plus a little sugar
Salt and pepper
2 medium tomatoes, skinned and roughly chopped (see p41) or about 125g of chopped cherry tomatoes
2 spring onions, trimmed and finely sliced
6-8 roughly torn fresh basil leaves or 1 heaped tbsp of chopped parsley

While the rice is still warm mix in the oil and season with salt and pepper and a few drops of vinegar. When it's nearly cold mix in the chopped tomato, spring onions and roughly torn basil leaves or parsley. Mix together and check the seasoning adding more salt, pepper, vinegar or oil if you think it needs it.

Grilling is one of the best ways of imbuing your veg with satisfyingly charred, chewy flavour. You can either do it in a conventional grill pan, a barbie or – one of my favourite gadgets – a stove-top ridged grill which gives you a similar effect

GMVs...

Serves 2 in any of the recipes opposite

UNDER 15 MINUTES (PLUS EXTRA TIME TO SALT AUBERGINES)

The shorthand is a bit of a family joke. My eldest daughter had an aversion to aubergines and peppers so we used to refer to them as GMVs – Grilled Mediterranean Vegetables. Fortunately, she now likes them as they make a versatile basis for all kinds of meals. You may well want to double the quantities here.

1 medium aubergine (about 300g)
2 medium sized courgettes
1 red or yellow pepper, seeded and quartered
About 2 tbsp olive oil
Salt and pepper

Wipe the aubergine and courgettes clean and cut them into thick, diagonal slices. Sprinkle them with salt and leave for 30 minutes to get rid of any bitter juices (you can skip this stage, if you like, but you get a slightly better result if you do it). Rinse them under cold running water and pat them dry with kitchen towel. Turn the grill on to its highest setting. Lay all the veg in a foil-lined grill pan, pour over a couple of tablespoons of olive oil and rub it into the veg with your hands. Season with salt and pepper. Grill the veg under a high heat for about 8-10 minutes until soft, and charred, turning them half way through.

- An alternative method would be to heat a ridged grill pan until really hot (about 3-4 minutes). Smear the aubergine slices with oil and place on the grill. Cook for about 2 minutes each side. Repeat with the courgettes and then the peppers, pressing the latter down well with a spatula. The upside is that you get sexy dark lines on the veg which look (and taste) as if you've barbecued them. The downside is that it creates a fair amount of smoke which may set off a smoke alarm.
- You could also add other veg like peeled and quartered onions, mushrooms or green peppers (though the latter don't have such a sweet flavour as the red or yellow kind).

...AND 3 WAYS TO SERVE THEM

Hot with Haloumi
Marinate about 125g of thickly sliced Haloumi cheese for 30 minutes with the juice of half a lemon whisked with 2 tbsp olive oil and seasoned with salt, pepper, a small crushed clove of garlic and a pinch of dried oregano or thyme if you have some. Lay the veg out in the grill pan as described above, tip in the cheese and the marinade and mix together well. (You don't need the additional olive oil.) Good with instant couscous.

Warm with basil and goats' cheese
When you've finished grilling the veg pour over a little extra olive oil and a few drops of balsamic or wine vinegar and toss together. Leave for 10-15 minutes then crumble over some goats' cheese (about 50g for this amount of veg) or other mild white crumbly cheese such as Cheshire or Wensleydale. Top with a few torn fresh basil leaves or a tablespoon of chopped parsley. Good with crusty bread or pitta bread.

Cold with hummus and pitta
In the unlikely event that you have any leftover grilled veggies they taste fantastic the next day (or a few hours later) stuffed in a warmed, split pitta bread generously spread with hummus – or houmous if you spell it that way.

PORTABELLA MUSHROOM 'STEAKS' WITH GARLIC AND PARSLEY BUTTER
Serves 2 **30 MINUTES – 1 HOUR**

When the desire for something substantial and meaty threatens to overwhelm you this is the recipe to go for. You could easily cook it in a mini-oven if you haven't got a full-size one.

4 large, flat portabella mushrooms
  (about 400g in total)
1/3 of a pack (about 85g) soft butter
2 garlic cloves
3 heaped tbsp finely chopped parsley
2 tbsp olive oil
Salt and pepper

Set the oven to 200C/400F/Gas 6. Wipe the mushrooms and cut off the stalks with a sharp knife. Mash the butter in a bowl with the crushed garlic and finely chopped parsley and season with salt and pepper. Pour 1 tbsp of the olive oil in a baking dish large enough to take the mushrooms in a single layer. Lay out the mushrooms, stalks upward. Divide the garlic butter between the mushrooms, spreading it evenly inside the cups. Drizzle the remaining olive oil over the edges of the mushrooms then bake for about 25-30 minutes until they are cooked through. This goes well with fried potatoes and a salad.

It's easy to get in a tomato and cucumber-fixated rut with salads but they should be just as varied as your cooked meals. The trick is to look at anything as a potential salad ingredient – leftover pasta, some grilled veggies or other cold cooked vegetables, fruit or nuts. Of course there are plenty of pre-prepared salads which will save you the time and trouble but salads don't take that well to being prepared several days ahead and you pay for the convenience. The same applies to salad dressings. Shop bought ones are more expensive and never taste as fresh as one you've made yourself. What you will need is a decent bottle of olive oil (which you'll probably have to keep in your room to stop your housemates using it for their late night fry-ups) and some wine vinegar.

The Free-Pour Method
A flashy way of dressing a mixed leaf or lettuce salad that is sure to impress any onlookers. It'll probably take you one or two tries to get the balance of ingredients right but it saves faffing around measuring things. The technique is this: season the leaves lightly with salt and pepper. Tilt the oil until it inches up to the edge of the bottle neck then wave it from side to side over the salad so that a steady stream goes zig-zagging across the leaves. Do the same with the vinegar but hold your thumb part way over the bottle opening so that it can't come out too quickly. (Aim roughly for 1 part vinegar to 4 parts oil.) Toss the salad and taste. If it seems too oily or vinegary add a little more vinegar or oil respectively.

A CLASSIC 'VINAIGRETTE' Serves 1
UNDER 15 MINUTES

A more conventional way of making a dressing. The mustard gives it a thick, smooth consistency which clings well to salad leaves.

1/2 tsp Dijon mustard
A little salt and freshly ground black pepper
1 dessertspoon wine vinegar
4 dessertspoons olive oil

Shake the ingredients together in a jam jar or whisk the mustard, salt, pepper and vinegar in a bowl with a fork, then gradually add the olive oil, whisking as you go.

Variations to try
You could add a little garlic, snipped chives or very finely chopped onion to the dressing (works well with bean or potato salads) or yoghurt as in the recipe below.

CHEESE, CELERY AND APPLE SALAD WITH YOGHURT AND HONEY DRESSING
Serves 1 **UNDER 15 MINUTES**

1 little gem lettuce or half a pack of iceberg lettuce salad
1/2 tsp Dijon mustard
1/2 tsp clear honey

1 tsp wine vinegar
1 tbsp sunflower oil or light olive oil
1 $1/2$ tbsp very lo-fat natural yoghurt
Salt and freshly ground black pepper
A good chunk (100-125g) Emmental or Jarlsberg
  cheese
2 sticks of celery, washed and trimmed
1 medium sized crisp apple (e.g. Braeburn)

Trim the base off the lettuce, break off the leaves, rinse under the cold tap and pat dry. Measure the mustard, honey and vinegar into a bowl and whisk together with a fork. Add the oil and yoghurt, whisk again and season to taste with salt and pepper. Remove any rind from the cheese and cut into small chunks. Trim the fleshy white base off the celery and slice thinly. Quarter, core and chop the apple and add to the dressing with the cheese and celery. Spoon over the lettuce.

ITALIAN-STYLE OIL, LEMON AND PARSLEY DRESSING
Serves 1 UNDER 15 MINUTES

A sharper dressing that, again, tastes good with mixed leaf and bean salads. The best type to use for tomato or olive based salads or salads using raw veg like fennel.

1 dessertspoon fresh lemon juice
$1/2$ a clove of garlic, crushed (optional)
A little sugar, salt and freshly ground black pepper

4 dessertspoons olive oil
1 tbsp finely chopped parsley

Put the lemon juice, garlic and seasoning in a bowl and whisk together with a fork. Gradually add the oil, whisking continually and stir in the parsley.

MIXED BEAN AND CRUMBLY WHITE CHEESE SALAD Serves 2
UNDER 15 MINUTES

An easy salad that makes a substantial meal.

A 400g can of mixed beans
2 spring onions, trimmed and finely chopped
  or 2 heaped tbsp finely chopped onion
100g Caerphilly, white Cheshire or Wensleydale
  cheese, cut into small cubes
1 portion Italian-style oil, lemon and parsley
  dressing (opposite)
Extra chopped parsley to serve

Tip the beans into a sieve or colander and rinse well under the cold tap. Shake off the excess water and put in a bowl. Add the chopped onion and cubed cheese to the salad. Pour the dressing over the salad and toss everything well together and sprinkle with extra chopped parsley. Good with warm pitta bread.

If you really want to add variety to your salads – and cut down the calories – play around with Asian ingredients. You don't need as much oil as you do with a conventional Western dressing, particularly if you use sesame oil. You can use more vinegar if you go for rice vinegar, which is sweeter and less sharp than wine vinegar. Soy takes the place of salt.

QUICK SPICY BEANSPROUT SALAD

Serves 1 Ve
UNDER 15 MINUTES

Asian-style salads tend to involve lots of chopping, but you could make a really speedy one out of a pack of stir-fry veg. You do need to buy one that's as fresh as possible though, ideally one where the sell-by date is a couple of days away. Several of the other ingredients are optional – use what you have to hand.

1/2 a 300g pack of beansprout stir-fry vegetables
1 spring onion, trimmed and finely sliced (optional)
1 mild green or red chilli, de-seeded and finely sliced or a little chilli sauce
1 tbsp sunflower oil or light olive oil
1 tbsp rice vinegar dressing
2 tsp light soy sauce or 1 tsp dark soy sauce
1 tbsp lime or lemon juice
25g salted or unsalted peanuts (optional)
1 heaped tbsp fresh coriander leaves (optional)

Rinse the stir-fry veg in cold water and drain well. Put them in a bowl with the spring onion and chilli (if using). Whisk together the sunflower oil, rice vinegar dressing, soy sauce and lime or lemon juice, pour over the vegetables and mix together. Scatter the peanuts and coriander leaves over the top.

WARNING
NEVER SERVE PEANUTS OR OTHER NUTS TO ANYONE WITHOUT CHECKING WHETHER THEY'RE ALLERGIC TO THEM.

• You could leave out the peanuts and serve the salad instead with the Gado Gado Peanut Dip on p74 used as a dressing.

ASIAN-STYLE LOW-FAT DRESSING

Serves 1 **UNDER 15 MINUTES**

Organic sunflower oil may seem expensive compared to the regular kind but the taste is so much better.

1 tbsp organic sunflower oil
1 tbsp seasoned rice vinegar
1 tsp soy (note – not a tablespoon!)
A few drops of sesame oil (optional)

Whisk together the sunflower oil, soy rice vinegar, soy and sesame oil (if using). Season with salt and pepper. Serve with a crunchy salad, carrot salad or with cold noodles.

VIETNAMESE-STYLE QUORN SALAD
WITH LIGHT LIME DRESSING Serves 2-3
PREPARATION AND COOKING TIME:
30 MINUTES TO AN HOUR

Slightly more complicated than the other recipes this is nevertheless so delicious I had to include it. Save it for the weekend when you're not in a rush.

1 tbsp sunflower oil
225g packet Quorn pieces
Zest and juice of 1 fresh lime, preferably unwaxed (see footnote) or 1½ limes if your limes aren't that juicy
2 tbsp seasoned rice vinegar
1 tsp light soy sauce
1 large clove of garlic, very finely chopped
2 slices of onion, very finely chopped
2 small or 1 medium-sized mild red chillies, deseeded and finely sliced
½ tsp grated fresh ginger or a tsp of ginger paste (optional)
Caster sugar and salt to taste
1 heaped tbsp finely shredded mint leaves
2 heaped tbsp finely chopped fresh coriander leaves
2-3 crisp Iceberg lettuce, leaves finely shredded
110g piece of cucumber, deseeded and sliced into fine strips
2 small carrots, scrubbed and sliced into fine strips
25g roughly chopped, unsalted, roasted peanuts to serve (see p125)

Prepare all your ingredients before you get going. Heat the oil in a pan and fry the Quorn quickly on all sides for about 3 minutes until lightly browned. Tip into a shallow dish. Mix together the lime juice, rice vinegar and soy sauce. Add half the lime zest, chopped garlic, chopped onion, chillies and ginger (if using), check the seasoning, adding a little sugar, salt or extra lime zest or juice if you think it needs it, then add the mint and a tbsp of the chopped coriander. Pour over the Quorn pieces, turn them well in the marinade and leave for at least 30 minutes while you prepare the vegetables. To serve, arrange the shredded lettuce in a shallow serving dish, top with the cucumber and carrot and spoon over the Quorn and dressing. Sprinkle with the remaining tablespoon of coriander and with the chopped peanuts (if using).

WARNING
NEVER SERVE PEANUTS OR OTHER NUTS TO ANYONE WITHOUT CHECKING WHETHER THEY'RE ALLERGIC TO THEM.

• The reason for buying unwaxed limes is to get the zest in your dressing rather than the waxed coating. Unfortunately most supermarkets sell them in packs of 4 with lemons but you might be able to find them in a Thai or Chinese supermarket.

Other salads...
All Seasons Pasta Salad on p45, the Tomato, Herb and Rice Salad on p51, and Salads With a Twist on pp106-107.

Soups are one of the easiest and cheapest meals to make from scratch. And the most rewarding. All you need is some fresh veg, stock and a little oil or butter. Once you get in the habit of making them you can almost do it with your eyes closed. (But don't, obviously.)

You can go two ways depending on the equipment you have to hand. If you don't have a blender make a rough, chunky soup which simply involves cooking chopped veggies very gently in some butter and/or oil until they begin to soften, pouring in stock, bringing it to the boil and cooking for about 15-20 minutes until the veggies are soft. The other way – and this suits soups based on single ingredients like carrots, peas or spinach – is to blitz it with a hand-held blender or liquidiser. You'll also need something to thicken the soup – flour, potato or pulses.

You'll note these recipes serve more than one person. But it's not really worth making soup for less. And you can always save some for the following day.

LOVELY LEEK AND POTATO SOUP

Serves 2-3 🍁 (IF USING OIL)
15-30 MINUTES

This is one of my favourite soups which I make almost every week in season. Leeks and potatoes are a match made in heaven. You'll get more flavour if you buy leeks loose from a market stall rather than the squeaky clean pre-wrapped ones you find in supermarkets.

3 medium or 2 large leeks
  (choose ones with their green tops still intact)
A good slice (about 25g) butter or 2 tbsp olive oil
2 small to medium potatoes (about 200-225g)
$1/2$ tsp fresh thyme or $1/4$ tsp dried thyme (optional)
600ml hot stock made with 2 tsp Marigold
  vegetable bouillon powder or an organic
  vegetable stock cube
Salt and freshly ground black pepper

Trim off any roots and about half the green tops off the leeks, removing any really tough leaves. Cut half way down each leek lengthways and open up the leeks under cold running water to remove any grit or soil. Cut the remaining part of the leek in two then cut into fine slices. Put them in a colander and rinse again. Melt the butter or oil in a medium to large saucepan then add the leeks and stir. Turn the heat down, cover with a lid or a piece of foil and cook over a low heat while you prepare the potatoes (peel and slice them finely).

Add the potatoes (and the thyme, if using) to the pan, stir well, then cover and leave to cook for another 5-6 minutes. Pour in the stock and bring to the boil then turn the heat down and leave to simmer until the vegetables are completely soft (about 15 minutes). Take the pan off the heat and mash the vegetables with a potato masher or fork until you have a rough-textured soup. Check seasoning, adding salt and pepper to taste.

- You could sprinkle some grated Parmesan or Cheddar on the soup.
- See also Italian Bean and Pasta Soup (p38) and Big Chunky Soups (pp102-103).

CARROT AND CORIANDER SOUP

Serves 4 Ve
30 MINUTES TO AN HOUR

Carrots make really, really good soup. Try to use organic ones which have a fantastic flavour and still aren't that expensive.

2 tbsp sunflower oil, preferably organic, or other cooking oil
1 medium onion, peeled and chopped or a couple of leeks, cleaned and roughly chopped (see opposite)
4 medium or 3 large carrots (about 350g) peeled and cut into rounds
1 medium to large potato, peeled and roughly chopped
1 rounded tsp ground coriander or crushed coriander seeds
750ml vegetable stock made with 1 tbsp vegetable bouillon powder or a stock cube
Salt and pepper
Fresh coriander or parsley

Heat the oil in a large pan, add the onion, stir and cook over a low heat until soft (about 5 minutes). Add the carrots and potato and stir again. Cover the pan with a lid or a piece of foil and cook very slowly for about 10 minutes. Stir in the ground or crushed coriander and pour in the stock. Bring to the boil and cook for about 20-25 minutes until the vegetables are soft. Blitz the soup with a hand held blender or put it through a blender or a food processor. Return to the pan and check the seasoning. Add salt and pepper to taste and a little extra water if you think it's too thick. Serve sprinkled with chopped fresh coriander or parsley.

Tarting up ready-made soups...
Even posh chilled soups can do with a bit of zipping up and tinned ones certainly can. A good squeeze of lemon juice generally freshens them up then add a handful of chopped parsley or coriander before serving.

For other soups...
See Italian Bean and Pasta Soup (p38), Big Chunky Soups (pp102-103) and Sophisticated Soups (pp130-131).

Pitta bread, particularly wholewheat pitta bread, is one of the best, inexpensive breads you can buy. And one of the most versatile. You can not only stuff it, dunk it in dips like hummus and make brilliant croutons with it (see p109) but also use it as an instant pizza base. Always warm your pitta before using it either on a low setting in the toaster (easiest) or under the grill or in a dry frying pan.

Pitta pizzas

Not a pizza in the conventional sense because you don't put it in the oven. But good nonetheless.

CARAMELIZED ONION, GOATS' CHEESE AND WATERCRESS PIZZA

Serves 2-3   15-30 MINUTES

3 tbsp olive oil plus a little extra for the leaves
4 medium red onions, peeled and thinly sliced (about 400g)
15g butter
1 tsp balsamic vinegar (optional but good)
Salt and freshly ground black pepper
1-2 wholemeal pitta breads per person, depending on size (the pitta breads, not you)
100g goats' cheese, roughly crumbled
A bunch or small pack of watercress or rocket, washed and trimmed

Heat a large frying pan or wok and add the oil. Fry the onions over a moderately high heat, stirring them occasionally until soft and well browned (about 10 minutes). Add the butter and continue to fry, stirring for another 5 minutes. Stir in a teaspoon of balsamic vinegar (if using) and season to taste with salt and pepper. Toast, grill or dry fry the pitta breads on each side until puffed up and lightly browned. Top them with the onions and crumble over the goats' cheese. Serve with watercress or rocket leaves, drizzled with olive oil.

Other good toppings

- Stripped-Down Tomato Sauce (p40) or a stir-in tomato pasta sauce and grated Cheddar.
- Soft cheese and stir-fried peppers (see sauce for Basque Butterbean Stew p36).
- Stir-fried mushrooms with garlic and cream (see Mushroom Pasta 2, p42).

Pitta pockets

A slightly twee description, I always think, for what is basically a pitta sandwich. Just toast your pitta bread, cut it across the middle to create two fat 'pockets' and stuff them.

STUFFED PITTA POCKETS
WITH MEXICAN BEANS Serves 2-4

 15-30 MINUTES

This is an adaptation of an oddly named Mexican dish called 'Refried Beans' which isn't really refried at all. It's boiled (or canned) beans, fried up with onions and chilli. One tin makes a surprising amount – enough for a good meal with leftovers for the next day.

1 tsp cumin seeds or ground cumin
2 tbsp olive or other light cooking oil
Half a bunch of spring onions, trimmed and sliced
  or 1 medium red onion, peeled and roughly
  chopped
2 cloves of garlic, peeled and crushed
$1/2$-1 tsp mild chilli powder or a few drops of hot
  pepper sauce or a small fresh chilli, deseeded
  and finely chopped
1 large or 2 medium tinned tomatoes plus 2 tbsp
  of their juice or 2 fresh tomatoes, skinned and
  roughly chopped (see p41)
1 x 400g can of red kidney beans
2 heaped tbsp chopped fresh coriander leaves
Salt and lemon juice to taste
4 pitta breads
Any salad ingredients you fancy or have available
  – fresh tomatoes, sliced cucumber, iceberg
  lettuce or other salad leaves, raw onion...

If you're using cumin seeds heat a pan over a moderate heat and dry fry them for a couple of minutes to release their aroma. Tip them out of the pan once they begin to change colour and set aside. Add the oil to the pan and then the spring onions or chopped onion. Fry for a couple of minutes then add the garlic, chilli powder or sauce and cumin. Stir and add the tomatoes, breaking them down with a spatula or wooden spoon.
Tip in the beans, cover the pan and cook for about 5-6 minutes until the liquid has evaporated. Take the pan off the heat and mash the beans roughly with a fork. Stir in the coriander and season with lemon juice and a little salt. Leave to cool for 10 minutes. Meanwhile toast the pitta breads lightly and let them cool too. Halve the pitta breads and stuff with the fried beans and salad.

- Any leftovers make a great sandwich. Just toast the pitta bread lightly, cool, then stuff as above.
- Sliced avocado is also a great addition but only if you're going to eat it straight away.

Other fillings for pitta pockets
- Cold Moroccan Spiced Chickpeas and Spinach (see p38).
- Leftover dal.
- Grilled or barbecued veg with hummus (see p53).
- Fried felafel, fresh tomato, cucumber, sliced onion and lettuce and a dollop of garlicky yoghurt dressing (p72 of my previous book, *Beyond Baked Beans*).

Toast doesn't have to be 2 slices of Mother's Pride (or Tesco's best). It can contribute to a dish in its own right. Chunky slices cut off a crusty loaf are far more satisfying and filling than those thin, floppy slices of cotton wool bread you pull out of a plastic bag. Buy a bread knife and live a little!

BETTER THAN BEST EVER CHEESE ON TOAST Serves 1
UNDER 15 MINUTES

I've revamped this recipe from my first book – having come to the conclusion that I prefer it with good old British seasoning like brown sauce or mustard than with chillies. But the revolutionary technique which keeps the cheese gooey and the toast crisp is unchanged.

A good chunk (about 75g) mature Cheddar
    or Lancashire cheese
1 tsp flour
1 tsp brown sauce or $1/2$ tsp Dijon mustard
    or $1/4$ tsp English mustard
2 tbsp milk
A couple of thick slices of wholemeal bread

Grate the cheese and put it into a small saucepan. Mix in the flour and the milk. Heat gently, stirring, while you make the toast. As soon as the cheese mixture is smooth, stir in the brown sauce or mustard. Pour over the toast.

PAN-FRIED CHEESE AND ONION TOASTIE Serves 1
UNDER 15 MINUTES

Here's how to make a toastie without using a sandwich maker. Use decent quality bread, otherwise the whole thing will just be a soggy mass. This works well with a green salad.

2 medium-cut slices of wholemeal or good quality
    white bread
Soft butter or butter-based spread
4-6 thin slices of mature Cheddar cheese –
    depending on the size of your bread
1 small onion, peeled and very finely sliced
Freshly ground black pepper or a few drops of hot
    or mild pepper sauce

Butter both sides of one slice of bread and one side of the other slice. Lay the slice that only has one side buttered on a plate with the buttered side downwards. Top with a layer of cheese and a layer of sliced onion and season with pepper or pepper sauce, then place the other slice of bread on top. Heat a small frying pan over a moderate heat for about 2 minutes (without any oil) then place the sandwich in the pan. Let the bottom side cook for about $1^1/2$ minutes then carefully turn the sandwich and let the other side cook, pressing down firmly on the top of the sandwich with a spatula. Flip the sandwich over a couple more times till the outside is nice and brown and the middle deliciously gooey.

SEXED-UP TOMATOES ON TOAST

 Serves 1 **UNDER 15 MINUTES**

Tomatoes on toast can be quite a feast if you use good bread, ripe tomatoes, olive oil and balsamic vinegar – all affordable luxuries.

2 tbsp olive oil
2 thick slices of sourdough bread or traditional
   French country bread or wholemeal bread
   (see footnote)
3 medium-sized ripe tomatoes, halved
A handful of washed rocket or watercress leaves
   (about half a small pack)
Balsamic or wine vinegar
Salt and freshly ground black pepper

Heat a ridged grill pan or frying pan until almost smoking (about 3 minutes). Rub a little oil into either side of the bread slices then lay them down on the pan. Turn them after a couple of minutes then keep turning until nicely browned. Put them on a plate. Add a tablespoon of oil to the pan. Season the tomatoes with salt and pepper then put them in the pan cut side down. Cook for about 2-3 minutes then turn them over and cook for another couple of minutes on the other side till soft. Arrange the rocket or watercress leaves on top of the bread and lay the tomatoes on top. Trickle over a little extra olive oil and a few drops of balsamic or ordinary wine vinegar.

• It actually helps with this recipe to have a bread that's a day or two old. Griddled toast is also good for fried and scrambled eggs (see p64).

SUGARED PLUM TOASTS Serves 1
UNDER 15 MINUTES

Toast toppings don't have to be savoury – in fact this is a great way to serve the underripe fruit you so often find in supermarkets.

2 plums
A small slice of butter (about 15g)
1 dessertspoon of caster sugar
$1/4$ tsp cinnamon (optional)
2 thick slices of malt loaf

Stone the plums by cutting round the stone and twisting the two halves of the fruit in opposite directions. (If the plums are not very ripe that may not work – you may just have to hack away the fruit from the stone.) Slice or chop into chunks. Heat a small frying pan, add the butter then when the sizzling dies down chuck in the plums. Stir-fry them for about a minute and a half then sprinkle over the sugar and cinnamon (if using) and fry for another minute. Toast the bread and pile the plums on top of the two slices. Top with a dollop of Greek yoghurt if you have some. Or, even better, some vanilla ice cream.

Eggs are so central to a vegetarian diet that it's worth using the best you can afford. And the freshest. Sell-by dates are clearly stamped on the box (and in some cases on the egg) so there's no excuse! Keep them in the fridge.

I also feel it's important to buy free range eggs. The conditions in which battery hens are kept are totally inhumane and would shock you if you're not already aware of them. (If you want chapter and verse, look up the RSPCA site www.rspca.org.uk.). I would also buy organic eggs which do cost a bit more – but at least you have the assurance that the hens will have been fed a vegetarian diet. Even at 30p an egg it's not a lot to pay when two eggs will make a decent meal.

HOW TO COOK EGGS

Boiled eggs
Start with the eggs at room temperature (if you prick the base with a pin or special egg pricker it will lessen the risk of them cracking). Bring a small pan of water to the boil. Place each egg in a spoon and lower it carefully into the water. Boil for $3^1/_2$-4 minutes (medium eggs) and 4-$4^1/_2$ minutes (large eggs) for a yolk runny enough to dunk toast in. (A timer helps.) For hard-boiled eggs continue to boil for 10 minutes in total. Remove the eggs and transfer them to a pan or bowl of cold water. To peel, crack them gently against a hard surface and peel off the shell under running water.

Fried eggs
Heat a frying pan for a couple of minutes until moderately hot then add 3 tbsp (clean!) cooking oil. Crack the egg(s) on the side of the pan (or on the edge of a cup if you feel a bit nervous about it) and break the egg(s) into the pan. Cook for a couple of minutes then add a small lump of butter to the pan, tilt it, holding the handle and spoon the hot butter and oil over the eggs so the yolks cook thoroughly and the whites puff up.

Poached eggs
Not the easiest of techniques without a poacher. I've tried various different ways of doing it but I don't think you can beat the Delia method. Which basically is to boil a kettle of water and pour it into a saucepan or frying pan to a depth of 2.5cm (about half way up the spoon bit of a teaspoon). Put the pan over a low to moderate heat and when the water looks as if it's about to boil (little bubbles will appear on the base of the pan) slide the egg in. (This is easier if you break it into a cup first.) Let the egg cook for a minute – the water should be trembling rather than boiling – then turn off the heat and leave it in the pan for another 10 minutes. Scoop it out with a slotted spoon, place it on a piece of kitchen towel to mop up the water then serve on buttered toast, spinach or whatever. The considerable advantage of this method is that you can; a) poach more than one egg at once; b) the egg white doesn't go flying all over the place like it does when you attempt to slip it into fast-boiling water (provided

your egg is scrupulously fresh – very important, that); and, c) it doesn't taste of salt or vinegar – the traditional additions to the poaching water. The one downside is that it takes 10 minutes. Can you wait? If not, fry it.

Scrambled eggs

Break 2 large fresh eggs into a bowl and beat them with a fork. Add a little milk and season with salt and pepper. Place a small, preferably non-stick, pan on a gas or electric ring, set on a very low setting. Add the butter and let it melt, then tip in the eggs. Stir them continuously till the mixture starts to solidify (anything from 3-5 minutes), then keep stirring till you have a rich creamy golden mass. Serve on hot buttered toast. (If you want to add mushrooms to your scrambled egg it's better to cook them first then set them aside, wipe the pan then make your scrambled eggs from scratch, otherwise you'll find you have dirty grey eggs, which will taste fine but just look pretty yukky.)

Separating eggs

To separate the yolk from the white of an egg, crack it against the side of a cup and let the white fall into the cup. Holding the two halves of the shell, transfer the yolk carefully from one half to the other, without breaking it, so that the rest of the white falls into the cup. Put the yolk into a separate cup or bowl.

PIPERRADA Serves 1
UNDER 15 MINUTES

A rather sexy spin on scrambled eggs from the Basque region of Spain. Don't be tempted to cut the cooking time or your eggs will go watery.

1$\frac{1}{2}$ tbsp olive oil
1 small onion, peeled, halved and finely sliced
A handful (about 75g) frozen sliced peppers
1 medium tomato (optional)
2 large or 3 medium fresh eggs, preferably free-range
Salt and pepper
1 heaped tbsp chopped fresh parsley (optional)

Heat the oil in a frying pan. Add the sliced onion and stir-fry for about 4-5 minutes until beginning to soften. Add the peppers, turn up the heat and fry another 4-5 minutes until beginning to brown. Take the pan off the heat, add the tomato (if using) and cool for a minute. Break the eggs into a bowl and beat lightly with a fork. Season with salt and pepper. Stir the eggs into the peppers, return to a low to moderate heat and stir until the egg is scrambled (about 2 minutes). Add parsley (if using) and serve with crusty bread or warm pitta bread.

• I like the mild sweet flavour of the onions and peppers but if you want it a touch spicier add a $\frac{1}{4}$ tsp of Spanish pimenton or paprika.

Omelettes and frittatas are basically the same thing except that a frittata has the filling mixed in with the egg and is generally left open rather than being folded over like an omelette. Although I often amalgamate the two techniques which I suppose is a Fromelette. Or an Omelettata.

MUSHROOM OMELETTE Serves 1
UNDER 15 MINUTES

There's a great deal written about how difficult it is to make a perfect omelette but don't let that put you off. It's a doddle really.

2-3 large fresh eggs, preferably free-range
Salt and freshly ground black pepper
25g butter
5-6 button or chestnut mushrooms (about 100g), rinsed and sliced

Crack the eggs into a bowl and beat them with a fork till the yolks and whites are well amalgamated. Add salt, pepper and a dessertspoon of water and beat again. Heat a small non-stick frying pan and add half the butter. When it starts foaming tip in the mushrooms and stir-fry them for about 3 minutes until beginning to brown. Scoop them out of the pan, wipe the pan with a scrunched up piece of kitchen towel and place it back on the heat. Add the remaining butter and pour the beaten egg into the pan. Working quickly, keep lifting the egg away from the edges of the pan so that the liquid egg runs underneath and solidifies. When almost all the liquid egg has disappeared tip the mushrooms back onto the omelette, let it cook for another 30 seconds then with a plate ready ease a spatula under one side of the omelette and fold it over, tipping the pan as you do it so that the omelette rolls onto the plate. (Don't worry if it isn't very neat the first time you do it. It gets easier with practice.)

• You can put all kinds of other fillings in an omelette – grated cheese, tomato or fresh chopped herbs, for example.

SURPRISINGLY GOOD SPRING ONION AND BEANSPROUT OMELETTE
Serves 2 **UNDER 15 MINUTES**

This is one of those recipes that came about out of a desire not to chuck away leftovers. What do you do with half a bag of beansprouts? Turn it into a Chinese-style omelette.

1/2 bunch of spring onions (about 4-5)
1 tbsp sunflower oil (preferably organic)
150g washed beansprouts
2 tbsp chopped fresh coriander leaves
4 medium fresh free range eggs beaten lightly with 1 tsp each of light soy sauce and water, and a little pepper
Extra soy sauce for serving

Trim the top half of the green leaves off the spring onions and cut off the root. Cut them into quarters, lengthwise then cut them into three. Heat a frying pan for a couple of minutes, add the oil, then tip in the spring onions and beansprouts and stir-fry for a minute. Add the chopped coriander, cook for another few seconds then tip in the beaten egg. Lift the sides of the omelette away from the edge of the pan with a fork to allow the liquid egg to run through, then, when the egg is no longer runny, let the omelette cook for a few more seconds. Using a spatula or palatte knife flip the edge of the omelette furthest away from you towards the middle, then roll it towards you and out of the pan onto a warm plate. Cut the omelette in half and serve with extra soy sauce.

LEEK AND GOATS' CHEESE
FRITTATA Serves 2
UNDER 15 MINUTES

Not really that different in technique from the previous recipe but somehow frittata sounds better for this one. It's a really simple and delicious dish – one to make when you want to impress.

1 large leek or 2 medium leeks
100g slice of goats' cheese
4 large or 5 medium fresh eggs, preferably
   free-range
1¹/₂ tbsp vegetable or olive oil
15g (¹/₂ oz) butter

Salt and pepper

Prepare the leeks as described on p58, and wash thoroughly under cold running water. Cut the rind off the cheese and crumble it onto a plate. Break the eggs and whisk them together in a bowl. Season them with salt and pepper. Heat a large frying pan, add the oil, heat for a few seconds then add the butter. Once the foaming dies down, add the leeks and stir-fry them for about 4 minutes until they are soft but not coloured. Tip in the beaten egg, making sure it covers the base of the pan. Lift the omelette at the edges with a fork to allow the liquid egg to run through to the bottom. Once most of the egg has solidified scatter over the goats' cheese. Allow the frittata to cook for a further minute then fold it over and divide it in two.

• You can make this for 1 and serve the second portion cold the next day with a salad.

Couldn't resist the pun, I'm afraid, which will get me into trouble with my kids. Anyway there are some really fantastic spicy egg recipes, especially from India. Here are three, two from the Todiwala family who introduced me to the joys of Parsee egg cookery.

PARSEE-STYLE EGGS WITH POTATO, SPINACH AND CUMIN

Serves 2 **15-30 MINUTES**

This is possibly the best egg recipe in the world. It comes from one of my favourite Indian chefs, Cyrus Todiwala, who runs an excellent restaurant called Café Spice Namaste. I've added spinach because I like it and it's a good way of sneaking it into your diet but leave it out if you prefer.

3 tbsp sunflower or light olive oil
1 rounded tsp cumin seeds
1-2 small green chillies, finely chopped and seeded
2 cloves of garlic, crushed
1 medium onion (about 100g) peeled and thinly sliced
300g (10$\frac{1}{2}$ oz) new or waxy potatoes, thinly sliced
50g (2oz) fresh spinach leaves, shredded (optional)
2 heaped tbsp fresh coriander
4 medium fresh eggs, preferably free-range
Salt

You will need a large frying pan with a lid or a large sheet of foil. Heat the oil in a pan over a medium heat. Throw in the cumin seeds and when they start to pop add the chillies and garlic. Cook for a minute, stirring, then add the sliced onion. Stir for about 3-4 minutes until it begins to soften then add the sliced potatoes. Turn them in the pan for about 3 minutes until covered with oil and spices, season with salt. Add 75ml water then turn the heat down, put the lid on or cover with a large piece of foil and cook for 20 minutes, turning the potatoes half way through. Stir in the shredded spinach and coriander. Form 4 hollows in the potato mixture, break each egg into a saucer and slide into the dips. Replace the lid or foil, turn the heat up to medium again and cook for 4-5 minutes until the egg whites are set. Remove the potatoes and eggs with a fish slice or palate knife and serve on warmed plates with some pitta bread or naan and a dollop of spicy chutney if you have some.

INDIAN-STYLE EGG AND CHIPS

Serves 1 **UNDER 15 MINUTES**

This fantastically easy recipe is from Cyrus's wife Pervin and makes a brilliant snack. You need those thin matchstick-sized chips that really taste of potato, not the gruesome polystyrene-textured, extruded chip-shape ones. Most supermarkets do an own-brand version.

3 tbsp vegetable oil or other cooking oil
1-2 spring onions, trimmed and finely sliced
(optional)
1 large clove of garlic, peeled and finely chopped
1 heaped tbsp of chopped fresh coriander
A small pack of ready-salted thin,
matchstick-sized potato chips (about 50g)
2 fresh eggs, preferably free-range

Heat 1 tbsp of the oil in a frying pan and fry the
onions, garlic and coriander for a few seconds.
Add the chips, stir-fry for a minute then tip onto
a plate. Add the rest of the oil to the pan and fry
the eggs (see p64). Serve with the chips and
some spicy chutney.

HUEVOS RANCHEROS ('RANCH-STYLE' EGGS) Serves 1

UNDER 15 MINUTES

*This hearty Mexican breakfast dish is one of the
best ways of serving fried eggs. Think ketchup
plus. The tortillas might sound like an
extravagance but they make the dish, and you can
use the remainder with other toppings (see below).*

4 tbsp sunflower or olive oil
1 small onion, peeled and roughly chopped
1-2 mild green chillies and/or $1/4$ tsp chilli powder
or cayenne pepper
1 clove of garlic, peeled and roughly chopped
$1/2$ a tin of chopped tomatoes or (only if they're
really ripe) 3 fresh tomatoes
1 tbsp chopped coriander or parsley (optional)
2 large fresh eggs, preferably free-range
2 corn tortillas (optional but really good)
Salt

Heat a pan over a moderate heat, pour in 2 tbsp
of oil then add the chopped onion, chillies, garlic
and tomatoes. Stir well and cook for about
5 minutes until most of the tomato juice has
evaporated and the sauce is becoming jammy.
Season with salt then stir in the fresh coriander
or parsley (if using). Tip into a bowl. Rinse the pan
clean under the tap, wipe dry, then swirl round a
little of the remaining oil and wipe off the excess
with kitchen towel. Take one of the tortillas and
press down in the pan for 30 seconds to warm
it through then flip it over and cook the other side.
Repeat with the second tortilla. Lay them on a
large plate. Add the remaining oil to the pan then
fry the eggs as described on p64 and set them on
top of the tortillas. Spoon the hot salsa on top of
the egg whites leaving the yolks showing.

• Tortillas also taste good toasted with Black Eye
Bean Salsa (p39) and Black bean Chilli (p79).

Breakfast may be a word you don't want to hear or even think about but all the evidence is that it's one of the most important meals you eat, kicking your body and brain into gear and giving you energy for the day (see p21). Even if you're on the run it's worth grabbing a banana and a honey sandwich to eat on the way to lectures. If you've got more time just delay breakfast for an hour or so till you feel vaguely human then try one of these scrumptious recipes.

ALL DAY VEGGIE BREAKFAST
UNDER 15 MINUTES

Cooking a fry-up is more about timing than technique. Happily it's much easier and quicker to accomplish with veggie sausages than with meaty ones and bacon. For a real blow out I'd suggest...

2 large dark flat mushrooms
3 tbsp cooking oil plus a little butter if you're not a vegan
2-3 veggie sausages
2 medium sized tomatoes, cut in half
2 fresh eggs, preferably free-range

Rinse the mushrooms under cold water and pat dry. Pull off the stalks and cut the mushrooms in quarters. Heat a large frying pan over a moderate heat, add 2 tbsp of the oil then add the mushrooms, sausages and tomatoes for about 4-5 minutes, turning them over every minute or so to brown them. Transfer them to a warm plate. Wipe the pan then add the remaining oil, heat for a minute then add the eggs. Slip the butter or a little extra oil into the pan then when it stops foaming spoon the hot oil and butter mixture over the top of the eggs to set the yolks and puff up the whites. Remove with a spatula or slotted spoon and serve.

• For other hot breakfast ideas see 'All you need to know about eggs', p64.

CRUNCHY BROWN SUGAR AND CINNAMON PORRIDGE

Serves 1 Ve
(BUT ONLY IF YOU USE SOY MILK)
UNDER 15 MINUTES

Porridge is my all time favourite winter breakfast – comforting and sustaining.

100ml porridge oats (half a cup or just over a third of a mug)
200ml water
100ml semi-skimmed or soy milk plus a little extra for serving.
1 level tbsp demerara sugar
A pinch of cinnamon

Put the porridge oats, water and milk into a saucepan. Heat, stirring, until boiling, and then cook, stirring occasionally, for 3-4 minutes. Pour into a bowl, pour over a little extra milk, sprinkle with sugar and a pinch of cinnamon.

- To make porridge in a microwave, combine all the ingredients in a deep bowl and heat for 2$\frac{1}{2}$ minutes on full power. Rest for a minute, then stir before adding the extra milk, sugar and cinnamon.

SPICED FRUIT COMPOTE WITH HONEY AND ORANGE Serves 2-3

1 HOUR-PLUS (SOAK OVERNIGHT)

Dried fruit is an underrated way of getting your five-a-day, especially glammed up in this sophisticated fruit compote. Make it the night before for breakfast the next morning.

1 redbush teabag or an ordinary teabag
250g mixed dried fruit (available in bags at health food stores)
1 tbsp runny honey
1 stick of cinnamon or $\frac{1}{2}$ tsp ground cinnamon or mixed spice
2 cloves (optional)
Juice of one orange or 4 tbsp orange juice from a carton
A small carton of plain, unsweetened yoghurt

Put the teabag in a mug, top up with boiling water and infuse for 3-4 minutes in the case of the redbush teabag, about 2 minutes for the ordinary teabag then take the teabag out. Put the dried fruit in a saucepan, pour over the tea and another $\frac{2}{3}$ mug of water (you need about 375-400ml of liquid in total). Add the honey and cinnamon (and cloves, if using), stir and bring slowly to the boil. Simmer the fruit for 5 minutes then turn off the heat, cover the pan and and leave overnight. Before serving, remove the cinnamon stick and cloves, add the orange juice and a little more honey if you think it needs it. Serve each helping with a dollop of yoghurt.

- Redbush tea, also known as rooibos or rooibosch is a full-flavoured South African herbal tea that makes a good caffeine-free alternative to black tea.
- You could also stir in some sliced banana and/or some flaked almonds before serving.

Breakfast time is an ideal time to do your bit for Fairtrade – you can buy Fairtrade tea and coffee, Fairtrade sugar, Fairtrade honey and Fairtrade dried fruits and bananas. Even if you only buy Fairtrade products as a treat for the weekend you'll be doing your bit to help individual producers, growers and their families have the kind of amenities in terms of housing, health and education that we take for granted.

Summer is really the only time of year when we get properly ripe, inexpensive fruit in this country, so take advantage. A simple bowl of muesli topped with fruit and yoghurt is a great way to start the day. Here are some more adventurous alternatives.

FRUIT COUSCOUS Serves 2-3

Ve (IF YOU USE SOY YOGHURT)
15-30 MINUTES

I owe this recipe to a friend, Sarah Willes, who runs cookery holidays for children. It's a really neat idea which can be varied endlessly depending on whatever fruit are cheap and in season.

100ml orange juice and water mixed (about 70/30)
100g instant couscous (or measure to the 100ml mark in a measuring jug)
A selection of roughly chopped fresh fruit (see footnote) – about twice the quantity of the soaked couscous
1 heaped tbsp of chopped roasted hazelnuts (optional)
A pinch of cinnamon (optional)
Plain or soy yoghurt to serve
1 tbsp runny honey

Heat the orange juice and water in a microwave or pan until warm but not boiling. Put the couscous in a shallow dish or bowl and pour over the orange juice. Give a stir, put a plate on top of the bowl and leave it for 5 minutes to absorb the liquid. Then fork it through to fluff it up and spread it around to cool down. In the meantime wash and chop up your fruit. When the couscous has cooled (about 10-15 minutes) tip the fruit and any juices into the bowl together with the hazelnuts (and cinnamon, if using) and mix together well. Serve each portion topped with a dollop of plain yoghurt and drizzle over some honey.

- In summer use seasonal fruit like peaches, nectarines, strawberries, raspberries and blueberries. In early autumn plums, pears and grapes are good while in winter you could use satsumas or clementines and tropical fruit like pineapple, mango and papaya.

APPLE AND RAISIN MUESLI

Ve (IF YOU USE SOY YOGHURT)
UNDER 15 MINUTES

The combination of apple and rolled oats is a particularly good one so funnily enough this is better made with a cheap muesli than a flashy, expensive one. In fact you could simply make it with porridge oats and add extra raisins.

3 tbsp muesli
About 75ml (5 tbsp) pressed apple juice
   (see footnote), preferably cloudy apple juice
A few raisins
1/2 a crisp apple (e.g. Blenheim or Granny Smith),
   cored
Plain or soy yoghurt to serve

Spoon the muesli into a cereal bowl. Pour over
the apple juice, stir in the raisins and leave for
5 minutes. Grate the apple into the bowl and stir,
then add a little more apple juice if you think it
needs it. Serve with a dollop of yoghurt.

- If you haven't got a grater you can obviously just
  chop the apple up small but the texture of the
  grated apple is really nice.
- If you want a fruit juice that actually has some
  health benefits go for a pressed juice rather than
  one that is made from concentrate. The flavour
  will be better too.

STRAWBERRY ROUGHIE Serves 1
UNDER 15 MINUTES

*Roughies were an invention of my first student
book,* Beyond Baked Beans. *Basically they're a
smoothie for anyone who hasn't got a blender.
Which probably includes most of you.*

4 or 5 ripe strawberries
About 1 tsp caster sugar
2 tablespoons of plain, low-fat yoghurt
A handful of muesli (optional)

Rinse the strawberries and remove the stalks.
Slice them thickly into a bowl then mash them
roughly, sweetening them to taste with sugar.
Half-stir in the yoghurt, leaving it streaky. If you
want a bit of a crunch, sprinkle a handful of muesli
over the top.

- You can also give raspberries the roughie
  treatment – about half a 125g pack.

BANANA, YOGHURT AND HONEY ROUGHIE Serves 1
UNDER 15 MINUTES

1 ripe banana
2 tbsp plain, low-fat yoghurt
A little runny honey to sweeten
A handful of muesli (optional)

Peel and slice the banana into a bowl and mash
roughly with a fork. Add the yoghurt and a little
honey to taste (I'd suggest about 1 tsp). Mash
again and top with muesli as above if you fancy it.

The time you're most likely to eat unhealthily is when you don't feel like cooking and simply grab whatever comes to hand in the fridge. Some cut-up raw veggies and a delicious dip removes – or at least reduces – the temptation to binge.

LOW-FAT CHILLI AND ONION DIP

Serves 4   **UNDER 15 MINUTES**

Tastes really rich and creamy but it's surprisingly light in calories. (Quark is only 70 calories per 100g compared to over 400 calories for cream cheese.)

250g Quark
125ml semi-skimmed or skimmed milk
1/2 a small onion, peeled and very finely chopped
1 clove of garlic, peeled and crushed or 1 tsp
   fresh garlic paste
A good few shakes of Tabasco Green Pepper Sauce
Salt

Tip the Quark into a bowl, mash roughly then work in the milk until smooth. Add the finely chopped onion and crushed garlic, then season with green pepper sauce and salt to taste. Serve with strips of raw vegetables such as carrots, celery, cucumber and peppers. Breadsticks are also nice.

• Make it slightly less sloppy and spread it on crispbread or (slightly more sinfully) a baked potato.

GADO GADO PEANUT DIP Serves 4

 UNDER 15 MINUTES

This is based on a delicious Indonesian salad called Gado Gado – a selection of raw and lightly cooked veggies with a peanut dressing.

1/2 tsp vegetarian or vegan bouillon powder or
   1/4 vegetable stock cube
125g crunchy peanut butter (about half a small jar)
2 tbsp fresh lime or lemon juice
1 tsp soy sauce
1-2 cloves of garlic, peeled and crushed
1 tbsp very finely chopped onion (optional)
1 tbsp sweet chilli sauce or hot pepper sauce to taste

Put the bouillon powder in a measuring jug, pour over a little boiling water, stir then fill up to the 100ml mark with cold water. Tip the peanut butter into a bowl and beat in 75ml of the cool stock until you have a smooth dip. Add the lime or lemon juice, soy sauce, crushed garlic (and onion, if using) and beat again. Season to taste with sweet chilli sauce or a few drops of hot pepper sauce like Tabasco. Serve with strips of raw carrot, cucumber and fennel or celery.

WARNING
NEVER SERVE PEANUTS OR OTHER NUTS TO ANYONE WITHOUT CHECKING WHETHER THEY'RE ALLERGIC TO THEM.

- With extra stock added this makes a good dressing for a crunchy salad (see Quick Spicy Beansprout Salad, p56).

FRESH TOMATO SALSA Serves 2

 UNDER 15 MINUTES

The classic Mexican salsa fresca – delicious with tortilla chips! Only worth making in the summer when tomatoes are ripe – and cheap.

4-5 ripe tomatoes
$1/2$ a small onion or $1/4$ medium onion, peeled finely chopped
1 mild green chilli, cut lengthways, seeds removed and finely chopped
Juice of 1 lime
1 heaped tbsp chopped fresh coriander
Salt

Remove the tomato skins by making a small cut in the top of each tomato, placing them in a bowl and pouring boiling water over them. After a minute drain off the water and plunge them in cold water. The skins should come away easily. Finely chop the tomato flesh and seeds and place in a bowl with the chopped onion, chilli and lime juice. Season with salt and stir in the fresh coriander.

- You can make this with cherry tomatoes in which case you don't need to remove the skins.

GUACAMOLE Serves 2

 UNDER 15 MINUTES

Another great Mexican dip. Good on its own – even better with the fresh tomato salsa.

1 large ripe avocado
1 tbsp lime juice
$1/2$ a small onion, peeled and finely chopped
A small mild green chilli, deseeded and finely chopped or 1 tsp of green pepper sauce
1 small clove of garlic, peeled and crushed
2 tsp olive oil
1 ripe tomato, skinned, seeded and finely chopped (see previous recipe)
1 heaped tbsp chopped fresh coriander
Salt and pepper

Cut round the avocado with a sharp knife then twist the two halves in different directions. Remove the stone and scoop the flesh into a bowl. Mash with a fork until you have a chunky paste. Pour over the lime juice then add the finely chopped onion, chilli, crushed garlic and olive oil and mix in well. Season with black pepper and extra salt if you think it needs it. Stir in the chopped tomatoes and fresh coriander.

- Avocado discolours quickly so try and eat this as soon as possible after making it.
- For other dips see Go Greek pp118-119.

SHARING

There's no doubt about it: the best way to save money is to pool your resources and cook a meal for four (or more) rather than one. So why don't more people do it? Simple. Natural resistance to being organised into rotas. You're never all in the same place at the same time. Some of your housemates are crap at cooking (and paying up). The same people end up doing it all the time... the reasons are endless.

But try. Think about it: £1 doesn't go a long way if you're cooking for yourself but £4 is more than enough to base a decent meal on. Three nights out of four you won't have to cook at all. And you'll eat more healthily and enjoy it more if you all sit round a table together.

Don't let the fact that your housemates aren't veggie put you off. Most meat eaters would prefer a home-cooked vegetarian meal to a meat-based ready-meal. They can always add some meat to what you've cooked.

This section has lots of everyday options. Just give them a go.

Even people who say they don't like spicy food end up succumbing to chilli. It's one of those reliable staples you want to master like shepherd's pie and spag bol. The critical ingredient to buy is some mild chilli powder (though I usually add some ground cumin too).

A CLASSIC VEGGIE CHILLI Serves 4

 15-30 MINUTES

Exactly like chilli con carne in every respect other than that it doesn't contain meat.

2 tbsp sunflower or vegetable oil
A 225g pack of Quorn mince or about 300g
   frozen Vegemince
1 heaped tbsp concentrated tomato purée
   (you can buy it in tubes)
1-2 cloves of garlic, crushed or finely chopped
   or 1-2 tsp fresh garlic paste
1 tsp oregano or herbes de Provence
1 tbsp mild chilli powder
1/2 tsp cumin (optional)
1 400g can chopped or whole tomatoes
2 x 400g cans of red kidney beans
Sour cream (optional)
Fresh parsley or coriander (optional)
Salt and pepper

Heat a frying pan over a moderately high heat for 2-3 minutes. Add the oil and stir in the soy mince or Quorn. Fry for a minute then add the tomato paste and stir until it's thoroughly mixed into the soy mince. Add the garlic or garlic paste, herbs, spices and tinned tomatoes (breaking them up with a fork if they are whole). Season with salt and pepper, bring to a simmer then turn the heat right down and simmer for 10 minutes. Drain the kidney beans into a sieve and rinse under cold running water. Add the beans to the mince and heat through thoroughly for the flavours to amalgamate (another 10 minutes). Serve on its own or with a dollop of sour cream and some chopped parsley or coriander. It goes well with baked potatoes.

How to tart up tinned chilli

• You can of course buy chilli in a can, though I tend to find that they're slightly too hot and the veg are too soft. You can generally improve them by adding half a can of drained, rinsed red kidney beans and maybe a handful of frozen peppers or green beans (just simmer them in the sauce till they're tender). Sharpen up the seasoning with lemon juice and a couple of tablespoons of chopped herbs (my remedy for everything).

BLACK BEAN CHILLI Serves 4

 **(IF YOU DON'T USE SOUR CREAM)**
1 HOUR-PLUS

This is my favourite chilli – good enough for a feast. It really is worth making with dried beans rather than canned ones but you need to remember to soak them at least 5 hours in advance, or, even better, the night before.

250g pack dried black beans or, if you want to speed up the whole process 2 x 400g cans black beans, borlotti beans or red kidney beans
1 green pepper (optional)
3 tbsp sunflower or olive oil
2 medium onions, peeled and thinly sliced
2 large cloves of garlic, peeled and roughly chopped
2 level tsp mild chilli powder
$\frac{1}{2}$ rounded tsp cumin powder (optional)
1 400g can whole or chopped tomatoes
Salt
3 heaped tbsp fresh coriander

Soak the beans overnight. Put them on to cook following the instructions on the pack. Meanwhile wash the pepper, cut into quarters, cut away the white pith and seeds and cut into chunks. Heat the oil in a large saucepan, add the onion and pepper and cook for about 7-8 minutes until beginning to soften. Add the chopped garlic and the chilli powder (and cumin, if using), stir, cook for a minute then add the tomatoes and stir again. Turn the heat down, cover and leave to simmer slowly while the beans carry on cooking.
(Or for about 15 minutes if using canned beans.)
Drain the beans, add to the tomato mixture, stir, replace the lid and cook for another 10-15 minutes to let the flavours amalgamate. Just before serving check the seasoning, adding salt to taste and stir in the fresh coriander.

Serve with as many of the following as you have time to prepare or can afford
- A small carton of sour cream.
- 1-2 avocados, peeled, stoned and coarsely chopped.
- $\frac{1}{2}$ a small pack (about 125g) crumbled white cheese (e.g. Caerphilly, Cheshire or Wensleydale) or goats' cheese.
- A pack of tortilla chips.
- A medium-sized red onion, peeled and roughly chopped.
- Half-baked sweet potatoes (see p86).

- Any cold leftover beans are really good as a filing for a pitta bread or a wrap. Not that you're likely to have any.

I'm in agonies of indecision as to where the apostrophe ought to go on this page heading. Two shepherd's pies? Two shepherds' pies. Or no apostrophe at all. Particularly as a shepherd's pie based on lentils can't really be said to be a shepherd's pie at all. You can shepherd sheep but you can't shepherd lentils. Hence Harvester's Pie which seems to me an altogether more appropriate name.

HARVESTER'S PIE Serves 4

 **(IF MASH IS DAIRY-FREE)**
1 HOUR-PLUS

If you're not a convert to lentils do try this.
It has a really satisfying meaty flavour.

2 tbsp light olive or sunflower oil
1 medium or 2 small onions, peeled and finely chopped or 150g frozen chopped onions
1 level tsp five spice powder
2 medium carrots (about 125g), peeled and roughly chopped
1 level tbsp plain flour
250ml stock made with hot water and 1 level tsp Marmite
1 level tbsp tomato ketchup
1 x 410g of lentils, drained and rinsed
Salt and freshly ground black pepper
1 batch of freshly made classic mash (see right)

First put your potatoes on to boil for the mash (see recipe below). Heat the oil and fry the onions for about 3 minutes until starting to soften. Stir in the five spice powder, cook for a minute then add the carrots and stir. Cover the pan and cook on a low heat for 6-7 minutes until the vegetables are soft. Add the flour, stir in the Marmite stock and bring to the boil. Add the tomato ketchup and the lentils and simmer for 5 minutes. Check the seasoning, adding a little salt if you think it needs it and some freshly ground black pepper and spoon the filling into an ovenproof dish. Preheat the oven to 190C/375F/Gas 5. Once the potatoes are cooked, drain and mash them as described below, and spread them evenly over the pie with a fork, roughing up the surface to make it look appealingly rustic. Bake for 25-30 minutes until the top of the potato is well browned.
Serve with ketchup.

CLASSIC MASH Serves 4

UNDER 30 MINUTES

750g King Edward or other good boiling potatoes
A good slice (about 25g) of butter
50-75ml warm milk
Salt and freshly ground black pepper

Peel the potatoes and halve or quarter them so you have even sized pieces. Put them in a saucepan of cold water and bring them to the boil (about 5 minutes). Skim off any froth, season them with salt then cook them for about 20 minutes until you can put the tip of a knife into them without any resistance. Drain the potatoes thoroughly in a colander then return them to the pan and put it back over the heat for a few seconds to dry up any excess moisture.

Take the pan off the heat, chop the potatoes up roughly with a knife then mash them with a potato masher or a fork until they are smooth and lump free. Beat in the butter and enough milk to make a soft but not sloppy consistency. Season with salt and freshly ground black pepper.

- For a dairy-free version replace the butter with olive oil or non-dairy spread and the milk with soy or rice milk or a little of the water in which you boiled the potatoes.

CHEESE-CRUSTED VEGGIE SHEPHERD'S PIE

Serves 4 1 HOUR-PLUS

I'm not a big fan of meat substitutes but I know many are and this Mediterranean inspired pie is for them.

2 tbsp light olive or sunflower oil
1 medium or 2 small onions peeled and finely chopped or 150g frozen chopped onions
2 cloves of garlic, peeled and crushed
1 small (200g) tin of tomatoes or ½ a 400g can of tomatoes
1 level tsp dried oregano
1 level tbsp plain flour
175ml stock made with 1 level tsp Marmite
250g frozen Vegemince or a 225g pack of Quorn mince
100g frozen peas
2 heaped tbsp of finely chopped parsley (optional)
Salt and freshly ground black pepper
75g grated Cheddar cheese
1 batch of freshly made Classic Mash (see opposite)

First put your potatoes on to boil for the mash. Heat the oil for a couple of minutes in a frying pan or large saucepan and fry the onion for 3-4 minutes. Add the garlic, oregano and flour, stir, then tip in the tomatoes, breaking them up with a wooden spoon or fork. Stir and cook for a minute then add the stock and bring to the boil. Add the Vegemince or Quorn and peas and simmer for 5 minutes then take off the heat, add the chopped parsley (if using) and spoon the filling into an ovenproof dish. Preheat the oven to 190C/375F/Gas 5.

Once the potatoes are cooked, drain and mash them (as described in the previous recipe) and spread them evenly over the pie. Sprinkle with the cheese and bake for 30-35 minutes until the top of the potato is well browned.

If I'm cooking for four or more I prefer to bake pasta rather than boil it. Large quantities of boiled pasta always seem to end up either soggy or lukewarm. If you don't agree just double up the recipes in the Solo section. Otherwise try one of these.

ROAST MEDITERRANEAN
VEGETABLE PASTA BAKE Serves 4

 1 HOUR-PLUS

This is one of those infinitely elastic dishes you can play around with depending on which vegetables are cheap – and which you like or dislike. Leave out the courgettes, aubergines or peppers if you prefer. Add chickpeas instead of pasta. Top it with cheese at the end. Feel free.

5 tbsp olive oil
1 medium to large onion, peeled and cut into 8
1 medium to large aubergine, cut into large chunks
1 large red pepper, deseeded and cut into large chunks
2 courgettes, cut into rounds
About 4-5 fresh ripe tomatoes roughly chopped or a 400g can of tinned tomatoes
1 tbsp of tomato paste (if using fresh tomatoes)
2 cloves of garlic, peeled and crushed or finely chopped
250g dried pasta shapes

About 3 tbsp chopped parsley
Salt, pepper and sugar to taste

Preheat the oven to 190C/375F/Gas 5. Pour 4 tbsp of the olive oil into a large roasting pan and add the chopped onion, aubergine, pepper and courgettes. Season with salt and pepper, toss them in the oil and bake them for 25 minutes, turning them half way through. If you're using fresh tomatoes dilute the tomato paste in a mug or jug with 225ml boiling water, stirring well to mix it in evenly. Add the crushed garlic and tomatoes (and tomato stock, if using) to the baking dish, mixing it well with the vegetables and return it to the oven. Meanwhile cook the pasta for a minute or two less than the time recommended on the pack. Drain the pasta and mix it into the vegetables and bake for another 5 minutes or until the pasta is cooked through. Check the seasoning adding salt, pepper and a little sugar to taste (this will bring out the tomato flavour). Stir in the parsley and remaining olive oil and serve.

- If you're not vegan you can sprinkle Parmesan on the pasta once you've served it or top the bake with some grated cheese when you add the pasta to give it a crusty topping.
- You could make it spicier by adding 1 tsp paprika or a dollop of chilli sauce when you add the tomatoes.

MACARONI CHEESE WITH LEEKS

Serves 4 **UNDER 1 HOUR**

I hesitate to mess with macaroni cheese because it's so good as it is. But the delicate flavour of leeks isn't too intrusive and just gives it that extra edge.

2 medium to large leeks, cleaned and sliced
  (see p58)
3 tbsp butter (40g) plus a bit for buttering the
  baking dish
3 tbsp (40g) plain flour
A small (584ml) carton of milk
150g strong Cheddar, coarsely grated
350g penne or rigatoni
Salt and freshly ground black pepper

Cut the butter into chunks and melt gently in a medium-sized non stick saucepan. Add the leeks, stir well and leave them to cook gently for about 4-5 minutes until soft. Take the pan off the heat and stir the flour into the leeks and butter with a wooden spoon. Put the pan back on a low heat for a few seconds to 'cook' the flour and butter mixture, stirring it all the time, then remove it from the heat again. Add the milk bit by bit, stirring to amalgamate it completely before you add the next lot. (Don't worry if it suddenly goes very thick, keep stirring, gradually adding the milk.) Leave about 50ml of the milk in the carton for the moment. Put the pan back on the hob, increase the heat slightly then bring the milk gradually to the boil stirring all the time. Turn the heat right down again and leave the sauce to simmer for 5 minutes, stirring it occasionally. Bring a large pan of water to the boil, add salt then tip in the pasta, stir and cook for the time recommended on the pack. Just before the pasta is ready, stir half the cheese into the sauce and season with salt and pepper. Add the remaining milk if it looks too thick. Drain the pasta thoroughly and tip into a lightly buttered shallow baking dish. Pour over the cheese and leek sauce and mix it in well. Sprinkle over the remaining grated cheese. Place the dish under a hot grill for about 5 minutes until the top is brown and crispy. Or if you don't have a grill bake in a hot oven (200C/400F/Gas 6) for about 15-20 minutes until browned.

- You can substitute other hard cheeses, but make sure they're medium or strong in flavour. Lancashire is good or Red Leicester.
- If you want a straight macaroni cheese without leeks, just melt the butter, stir in the flour and carry on with the recipe. You could add a spoonful of mustard to the cheese sauce.
- Use this sauce without leeks to make a cauliflower cheese.
- See also p114 for lasagne.

With all the ready-made veggie burgers on the market I admit that it's unlikely that you're going to want to make them from scratch. But if you do feel inspired these two recipes are well worth it. The key is to use dried lentils or beans rather than tinned ones – they hold their shape better and have a lighter texture.

LEBANESE-STYLE LENTIL CAKES WITH FRESH HERBS AND LEMON

Serves 4 ♦ 1 HOUR-PLUS

Guaranteed to convert a lentil-loather.

250g green lentils
3 tbsp ground rice
2 tbsp olive oil
1 medium onion (about 100g), peeled and finely chopped
2 cloves of garlic, peeled and crushed
1 tsp each of ground cumin and coriander
4 heaped tbsp finely chopped fresh coriander or coriander and mint
1-2 tsp lemon juice, and 1 whole lemon
Salt and freshly ground black pepper
Plain flour, for coating
Sunflower or rapeseed oil for frying

Cover the lentils with cold water and bring to the boil. (Do not add salt at this stage.) Cook fast for 10 minutes then turn the heat down, cover the pan and simmer for another 15-20 minutes or until the lentils are soft. Drain the lentils in a colander, return to the pan, mix in the ground rice, cover and set aside for about 20 minutes to cool and absorb the remaining moisture. Meanwhile heat the olive oil in a pan over a moderate heat and add the chopped onion. Fry gently for about 5-6 minutes until soft then add the crushed garlic, cumin and coriander. Tip the onion mixture into the lentils then whizz the mixture with a hand-held blender until smooth. Add the chopped herbs, season with the lemon juice, salt and pepper and mix well. Divide the mixture into 8 then roll each portion into a ball. Flatten slightly to form a small burger. Lay them on a baking tray, cover them with cling-film and chill them in the fridge for at least 30 minutes, preferably longer. When ready to cook, put a little flour in a bowl and dip each side of the lentil cakes in it, shaking off the surplus. Heat about 4 tbsp of oil in a frying pan and fry the cakes for about 2 minutes each side or until hot through. (You may need to do this in two batches.) Serve with lemon wedges and a mixed salad.

HOMAGE TO THE SPICY BEANBURGER

Serves 4-6 1 HOUR-PLUS

A vegetarian classic with a spicy twist.

250g dried red kidney beans, soaked in cold
    water for at least 5 hours or overnight
2 medium onions (about 100g each)
2 bayleaves plus a few black peppercorns if
    you have them
3 tbsp olive oil or other cooking oil
1 small green pepper, quartered, deseeded and
    finely chopped
2 large cloves of garlic, peeled and crushed
1$\frac{1}{2}$ tsp mild chilli powder
1 tsp ground cumin
1 tbsp tomato paste, ketchup or passata
1 medium egg, lightly beaten
100g fine cornmeal (polenta), plus extra for
    coating the burgers
3 heaped tbsp chopped fresh coriander leaves
Salt to taste

Drain the beans, put them in a large saucepan
and cover with fresh water. Add one of the onions,
peeled and quartered and the bayleaves and
peppercorns if you have some, but no salt
(it toughens the beans). Bring them to the boil, skim
off any scum and boil hard and fast for 10 minutes
(see footnote). Turn the heat down slightly and
continue to boil for another hour or so until the

beans are soft. Drain and remove the bayleaves.
Peel, halve and finely chop the remaining onion.
Heat the oil in a frying pan and fry the onion and
pepper for about 5-6 minutes until soft. Add the
garlic, chilli powder and ground cumin, stir and fry
for a minute. Tip half the mixture into the beans, add
the tomato purée or ketchup then whizz them up
with a hand-held blender or in a food processor.
Add the remaining onions and peppers, the beaten
egg and the cornmeal and mix together thoroughly.
Check the seasoning, adding salt to taste – you'll
need quite a bit. Finally stir in the chopped coriander.
Leave the mixture until completely cool. Put a little
cornmeal into a shallow bowl. Take a heaped
dessertspoon of the bean mixture, roll it gently into
a ball, dip it into the cornmeal and flatten it to make
a small patty. Repeat with the remaining mixture –
you should get 18-20. Lay them on a couple of
baking sheets and chill for at least 30 minutes.
Heat about 3 tbsp of oil in a frying pan and fry
a batch of beanburgers for about 2 minutes each
side. Drain on kitchen paper, keep warm and
repeat with the remaining patties. Serve with a fresh
tomato salsa (see p75) or chutney and a salad.

• It's important to boil red kidney beans hard at
  the start of the cooking process otherwise they
  can be poisonous.

86 HALF-BAKED POTATOES

I've already railed against the ubiquitous baked potato which is all too often some gigantic sodden football of a vegetable stuffed with gluey cheese. Despite its status as a fast food it's not particularly quick to cook – its only virtue is that it's cheap and filling. But I realise I'm in a minority so I've come up with a way of streamlining the task for you baked potato addicts. May I present the half-baked potato:

HALF-BAKED POTATOES 1

 30 MINUTES – 1 HOUR

Or I suppose, as they should more accurately be called, baked-half potatoes. They're halfway between a baked potato and a roast one but faster and less fattening than either.

1-2 medium-sized potatoes (about 250g) per person
Olive oil
Sea salt

Pre-heat the oven to 200C/400F/Gas 6.
Wash the potatoes and scrub them if necessary to get rid of the dirt. Cut them in half lengthways. Pour a little oil into a large roasting tin and place the potatoes in it, skin side down. Trickle a little more oil over the tops and rub it into the potatoes so they're well coated. Sprinkle them with salt. Bake for 30 minutes then turn the potatoes cut side up, drizzle with a little more oil if necessary and sprinkle with salt again. Return to the oven for another 15 minutes or until completely soft.

Other half-baked ideas
- Crispy potato wedges: same method as above. Just cut the potatoes into quarters or sixths. They'll take a little less time, about 40 minutes. You could also chuck in a few garlic cloves or sprigs of fresh rosemary.
- Chunky oven chips. Much healthier, tastier and cheaper than shop-bought ones. Just cut the potatoes into chunky chips and follow the master recipe. Cook for about 30 minutes.
- Oven-fried sauté potatoes. Is there no end to the versatility of this recipe? Cut the potatoes into thick rounds, rub them with oil and lay them in a single layer on a baking tray. They'll take about 25 minutes. Turn them half way through.
- You can adapt any of the above ideas to sweet potatoes though I think they benefit from a bit of chilli seasoning in addition to the salt – flakes or powder.

HALF BAKED POTATOES 2
UNDER 1 HOUR

These taste more like conventional baked potatoes but need less cooking time. Basically you start the potatoes in the microwave, cooking them for about half the time recommended in the instruction manual which will depend on your microwave and the number of potatoes you're trying to cook (probably around 6-8 minutes for four potatoes). Remember to prick them first and wrap each one in a sheet of kitchen towel. Then remove the towel, put them on a lightly oiled baking tray and finish them off in a hot oven (200C/400F/Gas 6) for about 20-25 minutes to crisp up the skin. Cut them open and stuff them with whatever filling grabs you: grated Cheddar, soft cheese with herbs and garlic, stir-fried onions and peppers, baked beans....

DOUBLE BAKED POTATOES
(AKA CRISPY POTATO SKINS)
1 HOUR-PLUS

If the entire point of having baked potatoes is to eat the skin here's a way of enjoying it on its own. Use the leftover potato to make another comfort-food favourite, Bubble and Squeak (see p90) or Spiced Cauliflower and Potato (p94).

2 medium sized baking potatoes per person
Olive oil or sunflower oil
Grated vegetarian Cheddar
Sea salt

Pre-heat the oven to 200C/400F/Gas 6.
Prick the potatoes several times with the prongs of a fork then rub a little olive oil and sea salt over them, and bake them in a roasting tin (or tins) for about 50 minutes to an hour until cooked. Take them out of the oven, cool for 5 minutes, then holding them with an oven glove cut them in half lengthways with a sharp knife. Scoop out the centre of the potato with a teaspoon and save it, leaving a thinnish layer of potato lining the skin. Halve the potatoes again and lay the quarters back in the roasting tin. Season with sea salt and pepper, sprinkle with grated cheese and trickle over a little extra oil. Turn up the oven to 225 C/425 F/Gas 7 and return the potatoes to the oven for about 15-20 minutes until crisp. Serve with a mixed salad or Fresh Tomato Salsa (see p75).

- If you want even crispier skins you could deep-fry the potato skins in a wok (without the cheese). But that's a bit like eating a fried Mars bar....

Like pasta bakes, potato bakes make great comfort eating. They're also really cheap. Just forget all that anti-carb propaganda.

CRISPY CHEESY GARLICKY POTATOES

Serves 6 **30 MINUTES – 1 HOUR**

This recipe is based on one from a classic '70s vegetarian cookbook called The Vegetarian Epicure *by Anna Thomas. For some strange reason it was called Potatoes Romanoff – maybe because it included sour cream. I've used créme fraîche which is a bit lighter.*

1.5kg red potatoes (e.g. Desirée)
375g carton cottage cheese
200g carton low-fat crème fraîche
2 large cloves of garlic, crushed
A bunch of spring onions, trimmed and finely
   sliced
100g strong Cheddar cheese, coarsely grated
Salt and freshly ground black pepper

You will need a large roasting tin or baking dish. Preheat the oven to 190C/375F/Gas 5. Peel and halve or quarter the potatoes. Place in a large pan, cover with water and bring to the boil. Boil for 10 minutes, remove from heat and drain. Meanwhile mix the cottage cheese with the crème fraîche, garlic and sliced onions, and season with salt and pepper. When the potatoes are cool enough to handle cut into cubes and place in a large lightly oiled baking dish. Pour over the cottage cheese mixture and mix in carefully taking care not to break up the potatoes. Sprinkle over the Cheddar and bake in a pre-heated oven for about 30 minutes. Finish off if necessary under a hot grill to get a really crusty topping. Good with a green salad.

CREAMY GARLIC AND POTATO BAKE

Serves 4-6 **1 HOUR-PLUS**

This famous French potato bake (they call it Gratin Dauphinoise) is usually served as a side dish, but I think it makes a great meal in its own right served with a salad to make up for all that cream.

284 ml carton whipping cream
2 cloves of garlic, peeled and cut into thin slices
750g potatoes
25g soft butter plus a bit extra for buttering the dish
Salt and pepper
100ml semi-skimmed milk
2 tbsp fresh Parmesan

Heat the oven to 190C/375F/Gas 5. Pour the cream into a small saucepan and heat very gently with the sliced garlic. Leave to infuse while you peel the potatoes and cut them into very thin slices. Butter a shallow ovenproof dish and place a layer of potatoes over the bottom. Dot the potato with butter and season with salt and pepper. Repeat until all the potatoes are used. Pour over the warm cream and enough milk to almost cover the potatoes. Sprinkle over the grated Parmesan and bake for 50-60 minutes until the top has browned and the potatoes have cooked through.

- You could also add some fresh tomato between the potato layers. Skin and deseed about 4-5 medium tomatoes (see p41) then cut them into strips or small cubes.

FENNEL, ONION AND POTATO BAKE

Serves 4 Ve
1 HOUR-PLUS

Not all potato bakes have to involve cream or cheese. This is rather an elegant one that would also be good for a 'Show Off' meal.

2-3 tbsp olive oil
1 clove of garlic, halved
3 medium to large potatoes, peeled and very finely sliced
1 medium to large onion, peeled and very finely sliced
2 medium bulbs of fennel, trimmed and very finely sliced
Salt and freshly ground black pepper

300ml vegetable stock made with 1 rounded tsp vegetable bouillon powder or $1/2$ a stock cube

Pre-heat the oven to 190C/375F/Gas 5.
Lightly smear a shallow ovenproof dish with oil and rub the cut garlic over the surface. Lay a layer of finely sliced potatoes over the base, then top with half the onion and fennel. Drizzle over a little olive oil and season with salt and pepper. Repeat, finishing with a layer of potatoes. Pour over the stock, trickle over a little more oil, then bake for an hour to an hour and a quarter until the vegetables are completely soft, and the top of the gratin is well-browned. If the top appears to be browning too quickly cover it with a piece of foil, removing it about 15 minutes before the dish is cooked. About half way through the cooking time tilt the pan and spoon the juices over the potatoes.

- To get wafer-thin slices of potato you need a sharp knife – worth buying if you're into potato bakes.

Personally I think you can never have too many potato recipes. Here are a couple of really flashy ones and one to use up leftovers.

ROSTI Serves 4
15-30 MINUTES

This isn't the recipe to make in a hurry but it's so cheap, so delicious, so impressive and, once you've got the hang of it, so easy that I couldn't leave it out. Basically you par-boil the potatoes, grate them and then make a big potato pancake.

750g potatoes
2 tbsp of olive oil
A good slice of butter (about 25g)
Salt and pepper

Peel the potatoes and halve or quarter if large so that all the pieces are the same size. Put them in a pan, cover with cold water, bring to the boil and cook for 7-8 minutes. Drain, leave until cool enough to handle (about 10-15 minutes) then grate coarsely. Heat 1 tbsp of the oil in a frying pan, add half the butter and once it stops foaming, tip in the potato and spread evenly in the pan so it forms a flat cake. Season with salt and pepper then cook for about 7-8 minutes until the edges of the potato are crisp and brown. Melt the remaining butter then drizzle it and the remaining oil over the potato cake. Cover the pan with a plate and flip it over so that the potato cake lands on the plate then slip it back into the pan, cooked side uppermost. Cook for another 7-8 minutes, sprinkle with a little more salt then serve cut into wedges.

BUBBLE AND SQUEAK Serves 2-3
UNDER 15 MINUTES

Leftover potato is a cause for celebration because it enables you to make one of the most satisfying of dishes, a hash. Which is basically smashed up potato fried up with other cold or warm veggies. Here's the most classic version, traditional Boxing Day fare in our household but good at any time.

4 cold boiled potatoes or the scooped out insides of 4 baked potatoes (see p87)
An equal quantity of cooked cabbage – or even leftover sprouts
2 tbsp light olive or sunflower oil
A small chunk of butter (about 15g)
Salt and freshly ground black pepper

Roughly chop up the potato and cabbage, mix together and season well with salt and pepper. Heat a medium sized frying pan over a moderate heat, add the oil, heat for a minute then add the butter. Tip in the potato and cabbage mix and flatten into a cake with a fork or a spatula. Let it cook for about 3-4 minutes then start to turn the mixture over. Keep turning it every few minutes until the crispy bits on the bottom of the pan get well mixed into the hash – about 8-10 minutes in all. Good with veggie sausages.

- You can cook a little onion and garlic in the oil before you add the potato and cabbage but I'm not sure it improves it.

CHEESE, ONION AND POTATO STACK PIE Serves 6
1 HOUR-PLUS

A recipe for the more experienced cook, though once you get the hang of rolling out pastry it's a doddle. The perfect recipe for Sunday lunch.

1 x 500g pack of puff pastry
Some plain flour for rolling out the pastry
1 large mild onion (about 225g), peeled and finely sliced
2 medium potatoes (about 250g), peeled and finely sliced
225g matured farmhouse Cheddar, thinly sliced
1 medium egg, lightly beaten
Freshly ground black pepper

Preheat oven to 220 /425 F/Gas 7. You will need a lightly oiled rectangular baking sheet. Take the pastry out of the fridge 10-15 minutes before you intend to use it. Cut one half slightly bigger than the other. Roll the smaller half into a large rectangle and place it on the baking sheet. Lay a layer of sliced onion over the base leaving about 1.5 cm border round the edges. Top with a layer of cheese then a layer of potato. Repeat twice, seasoning each layer lightly as you go ending up with a layer of cheese. Roll the other half of the pastry out wide enough to cover the base and the filling. Brush the exposed edges of the pastry base lightly with the beaten egg then carefully lower the top onto the pie without overstretching it, pressing it down well at the edges. Trim and indent the edges of the pie (as described on p120). Cut three vertical slits in the top of the pie. Brush with the rest of the beaten egg. Bake in the preheated oven for 20 minutes then reduce the heat to 190C/375F/Gas 5 for another 30-40 minutes until well browned and cooked through. Leave to cool for 20-30 minutes before serving.

- If you find the thought of rolling out pastry a bit scary you could buy two packs of ready-rolled pastry – a bit more expensive but maybe worth it if you've never handled pastry before. You'll probably need a bit more filling though. Increase the amount of potato, onion and cheese by 50%.

Just because you're veggie there's no reason why you can't enjoy a traditional Sunday lunch. Be sure to cook the Yorkshire puddings separately though or they won't be properly crisp.

ROAST ROOT VEG WITH GARLIC AND ROSEMARY Serves 4

 30 MINUTES – 1 HOUR

This is one of the easiest and most delicious ways of cooking root veg, guaranteed to convert even a parsnip hater.

2 medium onions, peeled
2 medium to large potatoes, peeled
3 medium to large carrots, peeled
2 large parsnips, peeled
3 tbsp olive oil
A whole head of garlic
4-5 sprigs of fresh rosemary or 1 tbsp dried
  rosemary
Salt and pepper

Pre-heat the oven to 200C/400F/Gas 6. Cut the onions and the potatoes vertically in half, then each half into three wedges. Quarter the carrots lengthways then cut each piece into two. Cut the bottom half off each parsnip and cut into two then cut the fatter top half into four or six. Cut away the central woody core which can be tough. Lay the veg in a roasting tin or large baking tray. Separate the individual garlic cloves and crush them with a rolling pin, pestle or the heel of your hand. Scatter them over the veg. Spoon the oil over the veg and mix well so they all get coated (easiest with your hands). Season with salt and pepper and distribute the rosemary sprigs around the tin. Roast the vegetables for about 45-50 minutes, turning them halfway through.

SUPER-CRISPY ROAST POTATOES
1 HOUR-PLUS

If you want proper old-fashioned crusty roast potatoes you'll have to cook them in a separate tin and finish them once you've taken everything else out of the oven. So you can't do them AND the Yorkshire puddings. It's either/or. You also need to use old potatoes (i.e. ones that are suitable for roasting, not ones you've had hanging around in a cupboard for several weeks).

1.25 kg roasting potatoes
4-5 tbsp rapeseed or vegetable oil

Preheat the oven to 200C/400F/Gas 6. Peel the potatoes, halve or quarter them depending on how big they are and place them in a large saucepan. Cover with cold water and bring to the boil. Add a little salt, boil for 5 minutes then strain off the water. Put 4 tbsp of oil into a roasting tin and tip in the potatoes, turning them in the oil. Roast the potatoes for 45 minutes turning them half way through. Turn the heat up to 220C/425F/Gas 7 and continue to cook until the potatoes are crisp (about another 15 minutes).

MINI YORKSHIRE PUDS

UNDER 1 HOUR

Yorkshire pudding rises much better if you cook it on its own. It's also much easier to make small ones than one large one. A 12-hole deep muffin tin is perfect.

110g plain flour
$1/2$ level tsp salt
2 medium eggs or 1 large egg, lightly beaten
175ml semi-skimmed milk mixed with 125ml water
Vegetable oil

Sift the flour into a large bowl and sprinkle over the salt. Make a hollow in the centre and add the egg and about a quarter of the milk and water mix. Gradually work the flour into the egg with a wooden spoon until it is all incorporated, beating it briskly until smooth. Gradually add the rest of the milk, beating well between each addition. Pour the batter into a jug and leave in the fridge while you get the oven and pan ready. Heat the oven to 225C/425F/Gas 7 (about 10-15 minutes). Pour a little oil into the bottom of each hole in the muffin pan, then heat the pan in the oven till the oil is smoking hot (about 12 minutes). Take the tin out of the oven and put it on a heatproof surface like the top of the cooker or a wooden chopping board, and pour the batter half way up the holes in the pan. (It should immediately start to bubble up and sizzle.) Put the pan back in the oven and cook for about 20-25 minutes until the puddings are well browned and puffed up. Serve immediately.

FIVE SPICE ONION GRAVY

UNDER 30 MINUTES

Don't panic! I'm not suggesting you need to buy five different spices for this recipe simply that you use Chinese five spice which creates a fabulously savoury gravy.

3 tbsp olive oil or other cooking oil
3 medium onions (about 300-350g), peeled and sliced
$1/4$ tsp of five spice powder
$1 1/2$ level tbsp of plain flour
350ml of stock made with boiling water and a good tsp of Marmite
Freshly ground black pepper

Heat the oil in a large saucepan. Tip in the onions, stir well and cook over a medium heat for about 10-12 minutes until soft and beginning to brown. Stir in the five spice powder and flour and gradually add the hot stock, stirring it well as you go. Bring to the boil then turn the heat right down and simmer for 5 minutes or until ready to use it. Season with pepper to taste.

I could happily live on Indian vegetarian food – it's so amazingly varied. I also love the combination of dishes you get in an Indian restaurant – a curry, a rice dish, a dal, a chutney – the perfectly balanced meal. Of course you don't need to make all four – a curry and a pilau or a dal and rice would make a really satisfying supper.

AUBERGINE AND PEA CURRY

Serves 3-4
30 MINUTES – 1 HOUR

A delicious curry I've adapted from Hansa Dahbi's Indian Vegetarian Cookbook *published by Hansa, a Gujarati restaurant in Leeds. Don't be daunted by the number of spices – it really is very simple.*

4 tbsp sunflower or vegetable oil
1 level tsp mustard seeds
A 200g tin or $1/2$ a 400g tin of chopped or whole tomatoes or $1/2$ a 500g pack of passata
1 large clove of garlic, peeled and crushed
A small chunk of fresh ginger, peeled and grated
1 tsp each of ground turmeric, ground cumin and ground coriander
$1/2$ tsp chilli powder or crushed red chillies
1 tsp salt
350g frozen peas
1 large aubergine cut into chunks (see footnote)
3 tbsp chopped coriander leaves

Heat a large frying pan or wok for 2-3 minutes, add 2 tbsp of the oil then add the mustard seeds. Once they start to pop and colour take the pan off the heat and carefully tip in the tomatoes (watch out – they may splatter), the garlic and the rest of the spices. Return the pan to the heat and stir-fry for 4-5 minutes until the tomato begins to separate from the oil. Add the aubergine to the pan and fry it for 3-4 minutes, stirring occasionally then add the peas and 150ml of boiling water. Bring to the boil, turn the heat down, cover the pan and simmer for about 20 minutes until the aubergine is soft. Stir in the chopped coriander and serve. You can make this ahead and reheat it adding a little extra water.

• If you have time sprinkle the aubergine with salt and leave it for half an hour before you use it which will draw out its bitter juices. Then rinse and pat dry with kitchen towel before proceeding with the recipe as above.

SPICED CAULIFLOWER AND POTATO

Serves 4 **PREPARATION AND COOKING TIME: 15-30 MINUTES**

Think of this homey dish as the North Indian equivalent of bubble and squeak and you won't be far off track. It's ideal for leftover potatoes if you ever have any, otherwise make it from scratch. The pre-cooking of the veg is worthwhile I promise you.

About 250-275g new potatoes
1 medium sized cauliflower (about 500-550g once the leaves have been removed)
3 tbsp sunflower oil or other cooking oil
2 level tsp cumin seeds
1 large or 2 medium mild chillies, deseeded and finely sliced
1 large clove of garlic, peeled and crushed
1 small lump of fresh ginger, peeled and grated or 1 tsp fresh ginger purée
1 level tsp each ground turmeric, ground coriander or ground cumin plus 1/4 tsp chilli powder or 2-3 tsp of a mild-medium hot curry powder
3 tbsp chopped fresh coriander
Salt and a good squeeze of lemon juice

Boil a pan of water. Wash and scrub the potatoes if necessary. Put them into the water, bring back to the boil, add a little salt and cook for 10 minutes. Drain and set aside. Cut the base off the cauliflower then cut the florets off the stem and divide them up into smallish pieces. Put them into a saucepan, cover them with boiling water, bring them back to the boil and cook for 2 minutes. Drain. Heat the oil in a wok or large frying pan, tip in the cumin seeds and stir for a few minutes until they start to brown. Immediately tip in the cauliflower and stir-fry for about 4-5 minutes until it's nicely browned. Add the chillies, garlic and ginger, stir, then add the spices

and stir again. Cut the potatoes into smallish cubes and add to the pan and stir, then reduce the heat and cook the mixture for about 10 minutes, stirring to stop it sticking and to prise the lovely crusty bits off the bottom of the pan. When the vegetables are completely cooked add the coriander and season well with salt and a good squeeze of lemon juice. Serve with a dal and/or some naan or pitta bread. It also tastes good with Onion Raita (below), Fresh Coriander Chutney (p97) or a sweet, spicy chutney. (As this is a dry dish you don't need rice.)

• You could add a couple of chopped fresh, skinned tomatoes as well when you add the potatoes.

ONION RAITA Serves 4
UNDER 15 MINUTES

Simple, delicious and refreshing.

A small carton of plain, unsweetened low-fat yoghurt
A small onion or 1/2 a medium onion, peeled and very finely sliced
Salt
Chilli powder or paprika

Tip the yoghurt into a bowl, add the onion, stir well and season to taste with salt. If you've time leave for 15 minutes for the flavours to infuse. Sprinkle with a little chilli powder or paprika before serving.

I have to admit I wasn't a big lentil fan when I started this book. Now I really love them. Both of the following recipes can be made with a can of lentils which makes them particularly quick and easy. For other Indian recipes see the list of vegetarian recipes in *Beyond Baked Beans* (p191).

GENTLY SPICED LENTILS WITH TOMATO AND CREAM

Serves 4 (or 1, if you're as addicted to it as I am)
15-30 MINUTES

You might think this sounds an unlikely combination but it's a blissful one – good enough to eat on its own.

2 tbsp sunflower or vegetable oil
1 medium onion, peeled and finely sliced
2 tsp ginger and garlic paste (see footnote) or
  1 crushed clove of garlic and a little grated
  fresh ginger
1 1/2 tsp garam masala
A 200g tin or 1/2 a 400g tin of whole or chopped
  tomatoes or half a 500g carton of creamed
  tomatoes or passata
1 tsp tomato paste (if you have some handy)
400g can of brown or green lentils, drained and
  rinsed
25g butter at room temperature
2 tbsp single cream
Salt to taste

Heat a small pan for a couple of minutes over a moderate heat then add the oil. Fry the onion quite fast for 5-6 minutes, stirring occasionally until the edges start to blacken. Add the garlic and ginger paste and the garam masala, stir, then add the tomatoes or passata (and tomato paste, if using). Tip in the lentils, add 100ml of water, bring to the boil and simmer for about 10 minutes, stirring occasionally until the lentils become smooth and creamy. Stir in the butter and cream and season to taste with salt. Good with Pilau Rice (see p50) or Spiced Cauliflower and Potato (see p94).

• You can buy garlic and ginger paste from most Asian grocers.

CARROT AND LENTIL PILAU

Serves 2-3 on its own; 3-4 with a curry

 PREPARATION AND COOKING TIME:
15-30 MINUTES

Another surprisingly good lentil recipe, using a can. Again it makes a complete meal with some onion raita or fresh coriander chutney.

2 tbsp vegetable, sunflower or other cooking oil
1 level tbsp whole garam masala (see footnote)
  or 2 level tsp pilau rice seasoning or 1 1/2 tsp
  mild to medium hot curry powder
1 medium onion (about 100g) peeled, halved and

roughly chopped
1 medium carrot, peeled and coarsely grated
1 clove of garlic, peeled and crushed
100ml basmati rice (about 100g)
1 x 300g can of green lentils, drained and rinsed
Salt and lemon juice to taste

If you're using whole spices, crush them with a pestle and mortar or the end of a rolling pin, removing any hard pieces of husk. Heat the oil in a saucepan, add the spices and fry for a few seconds till they release their aromas then tip in the onion and stir-fry over a moderate heat for 2-3 minutes. Add the grated carrot and garlic, stir, then add the rice and fry for a minute or two. Add the lentils, a little salt and 200ml of hot water, give one more stir then put a lid on the pan, turn the heat down and simmer for about 10-12 minutes until the water has been absorbed. Turn off the heat and leave the pan for another 5-10 minutes. Check seasoning and add a little more salt and/or a squeeze of lemon juice to taste.

- You can find whole garam masala in Asian shops. Supermarkets also sell tubs and packets of whole spices but they tend to be more expensive.
- You could substitute other veg such as grated courgettes or add some fresh coriander at the end.

FRESH CORIANDER CHUTNEY
UNDER 1 HOUR (ALLOWING TIME TO INFUSE)

My all-time favourite Indian chutney.

$1/2$ a large pack or bunch of coriander (about 75g)
2-3 sprigs of mint
3 heaped tbsp plain, unsweetened low-fat yoghurt
1 clove of garlic, peeled and crushed with a little salt
1 chilli, de-seeded and finely chopped (optional)
1-2 tsp fresh lemon juice
A pinch of ground cumin (optional)
Salt to taste

Wash the coriander thoroughly, shake dry, then remove the thicker stalks. Chop the leaves as finely as possible. Wash the mint, strip the leaves from the stalks and chop them very finely too. Put the yoghurt in a bowl and mix in the mint, coriander and crushed garlic (and chilli, if using). Season to taste with salt and lemon juice (and a little cumin, if using). Cover and leave in the fridge for half an hour to let the flavours infuse. Eat within 2 hours of making it (which shouldn't be difficult).

- If you have a food processor or blender you can simply bung this all in together but don't overprocess it or you'll get something that resembles a pale green soup rather than a relish. Alternatively you can give it a bit of a whizz with a hand-held blender.

I'm always amazed how much food you can make with a comparatively small amount of rice or grains. 250g of pasta doesn't take you that far – enough for two decent servings, maybe three at a pinch. But the same amount of rice, pearl barley or couscous will easily serve four. And it doesn't take that much longer to cook.

GREEN RICE WITH (OR WITHOUT) BROCCOLI

Serves 4 Ve **PREPARATION AND COOKING TIME: 15-30 MINUTES**

This fresh-tasting healthy, herby, pilaf is a great recipe to make when you're really skint.

2 tbsp olive oil, plus a little extra to taste
A bunch of spring onions trimmed and sliced or
   1 medium to large onion, peeled and chopped
   or 125g frozen chopped onions
100g frozen peas
125g frozen baby broad beans
250g basmati or other long grain rice
600ml hot vegetable stock made with 2 rounded
   tsp vegan bouillon powder or a vegetable
   stock cube
4 tbsp chopped fresh parsley
Salt, pepper and 2-3 tsp of lemon juice
2 heads of broccoli, cut into small florets (optional)

Heat the olive oil over a moderate heat in a large saucepan and add the chopped spring onions or onion. Cover with a lid and cook gently for 3-5 minutes (3 minutes if you're using spring onions), then stir in the frozen peas and broad beans and cook for another couple of minutes. Turn the heat up, add the rice, stir and pour in the stock. Bring to the boil, stir, turn down the heat again and cover the pan. Cook for about 15 minutes until the stock is absorbed then turn off the heat, season with salt, pepper and the lemon juice and stir in the parsley. Leave covered for 5-10 minutes so that the rice fluffs up. Steam or microwave the broccoli (if using) for about 3 minutes until it's bright green and just cooked. Serve with the rice and a little extra olive oil (or butter if you're not a vegan).

- Broken basmati is about a third cheaper than the better, unbroken kind.

MUSHROOM BARLOTTO Serves 4

 15-30 MINUTES

This is one of my elder daughter's favourite recipes. Basically it's a risotto made with barley rather than rice so it doesn't need stirring. Or not much anyway. It's also much, much cheaper than risotto rice.

2 tbsp sunflower oil or olive oil
2 medium or 1 large onion, peeled and finely chopped
2 cloves of garlic, peeled and crushed
About 150g mushrooms, rinsed clean and roughly chopped
3 sticks of celery, trimmed and finely sliced
1 tsp each of ground cumin and coriander
$1/4$ tsp hot paprika or cayenne pepper
250g pearl barley
$1/2$ a 400g tin chopped tomatoes
Salt
About 4 heaped tbsp chopped fresh coriander leaves or a mixture of chopped coriander and parsley.

Heat the oil over a moderate heat in a large saucepan. Add the chopped onion, stir and cook gently for about 5 minutes until soft. Add the crushed garlic, chopped mushrooms, and celery and continue to cook for another 5 minutes, stirring occasionally. Add the spices, pearl barley and chopped tomatoes and stir, then pour in 500ml of boiling water. Bring back to the boil then cover, turn the heat right down and simmer for about 25-30 minutes, stirring occasionally until almost all the water is absorbed. Check seasoning, adding salt to taste then chuck in the chopped herbs. Stir and serve.

- You can also make a really nice barlotto based on leeks. Simply clean a couple of large leeks (see p58), soften them in a little oil or oil and butter, stir in 250g of pearl barley and 500ml of vegetable stock then cook over a low heat until the liquid has been absorbed. Stir in 3-4 tbsp freshly grated Parmesan and a couple of tablespoons of cream or crème fraîche and season with salt and pepper.
- See also Risotto p112.

Couscous is the new rice but don't bother with the pre-flavoured varieties which are almost universally overpriced.

BIG VEGGIE COUSCOUS

Serves 8 🍃

**PREPARATION AND COOKING TIME:
30 MINUTES – 1 HOUR**

This really is a great recipe – easy, tasty, cheap and filling. It takes a bit of time though so I'd make it at a weekend or on a day when you're not in a rush. Some elements – the onions, carrots and spices – are constant, others can be substituted depending on what's in season. You need about a kilo to a kilo and a half of veg in total.

3 tbsp olive, sunflower or vegetable oil
2 medium onions, peeled and sliced
2 level tbsp Moroccan spice mix (see p12) or
   2 tsp ground cumin, 2 tsp ground coriander,
   1 tsp turmeric and $1/2$ tsp chilli powder
1 level tbsp plain flour
$1^{1}/_{2}$ litres of weak vegetable stock made with
   1 rounded tbsp Marigold vegetable or vegan
   bouillon powder or a vegetable stock cube
3 medium or 2 large carrots, peeled and cut
   into even-sized chunks
2 medium or 1 large parsnip, peeled and cut
   into even-sized chunks
A small swede or $1/2$ a medium sized swede

A small cauliflower, trimmed and cut into florets
A 200g tin or $1/2$ a 400g tin of tomatoes or 3 fresh
   tomatoes, skinned and chopped or 3 tbsp
   passata or creamed tomatoes
1 400g tin of chickpeas, drained and rinsed
4 heaped tbsp chopped fresh coriander or
   coriander and parsley
Salt and lemon juice to taste
500g instant couscous
Hot sauce (or harissa, for authenticity) to serve
   (optional)

First get all your veg ready and chopped into even-sized chunks. Put them in piles depending on how long they will take to cook (root veg take longer than other veg). Heat the oil in a large saucepan or casserole and add the onions. Cook over a moderate heat for about 5 minutes then stir in the spices. Cook for a minute then add the flour, stir then gradually add the stock. Bring to the boil, add the carrots, parsnip and swede, bring back to the boil and simmer for about 7-8 minutes. Add the cauliflower bring back to the boil and cook for another 10 minutes or so until the cauliflower is cooked. Spoon off about 300ml of the cooking liquid with a ladle or mug, pour it into a bowl and add enough boiling water to bring it up to the amount you need for cooking the couscous (check the packet). Sprinkle the couscous over the hot stock, stir, cover and leave to absorb the stock. Meanwhile add the tomatoes or passata, chickpeas and coriander to the couscous, heat through and leave to simmer for about 5 minutes. Check the seasoning, adding salt and fresh lemon juice to taste. Fork through the couscous to fluff it up then serve in bowls with the vegetables spooned over the top. Offer hot sauce or harissa for those who like it hotter.

- The parsnips, swede and cauliflower are suitable winter vegetables. You could also use squash, or sweet potatoes. In the summer you could add turnips, courgettes, fennel, aubergines, peppers or green beans.

CUCUMBER, HERB AND COUSCOUS SALAD Serves 4-6

 PREPARATION AND COOKING TIME: 15-30 MINUTES

You can make a scaled-down version of this with leftover couscous but it's better made from scratch.

250g instant couscous
250ml light vegetable stock made with 1 tsp Marigold vegetable or vegan bouillon powder
5 tbsp olive oil
2 tsp fresh basil or coriander paste (optional but good – see footnote)
2-3 tbsp lemon juice
1/3-1/2 a cucumber
150g cherry tomatoes, halved
1/2 a small red onion, peeled and finely chopped
2 heaped tbsp finely chopped fresh mint leaves
2 heaped tbsp chopped coriander or parsley
Salt and pepper

Make up the couscous following the instructions on the packet but using stock instead of water and adding 1 tbsp of the olive oil. Once the liquid is absorbed fork the couscous through to break up any lumps and tip it into a shallow dish to cool. Mix together the basil or coriander paste (if using), 2 tbsp of the lemon juice and the remaining oil and season to taste with salt and pepper. Cut the cucumber into four, lengthways, cut away the seeds and chop into small pieces. Tip the cucumber, tomatoes, onion and herbs into the couscous, pour over the dressing and toss together thoroughly. Check the seasoning, adding more salt, pepper or lemon juice to taste.

You could also add/substitute:
- a handful of black olives.
- a few toasted pinenuts.
- some crumbled white cheese (like Feta, Caerphilly or Wensleydale).
- cooked peas or broad beans.
- chargrilled peppers or courgettes.

- Herb pastes are quite expensive but useful for zipping up a dressing or pasta sauce.

Soup never sounds very sustaining but if it's the kind you can stand a spoon in, it's just as satisfying as a plate of pasta. It's also one of those down-to-earth, unfussy meals that doesn't mind being left hanging around, so it's a good dish to make when everyone's coming in at different times. The one thing I would beg you not to use is an ordinary commercial stock cube – they'll absolutely wreck the taste of any veg you put in the soup. Do invest in a tub of Marigold vegetable (or vegan) bouillon powder. No, I haven't got shares in the company – I just think it's one of those products you can't live without, though an organic veggie stock cube would do fine.

CHUNKY ITALIAN VEGETABLE SOUP

Serves 6 **PREPARATION AND COOKING TIME: 30 MINUTES TO AN HOUR**

Or minestrone, if you want to give it its proper name. This is a formula you can vary endlessly depending on what veg are cheap and in season. It also reheats well if you want to leave some for the next day.

3 tbsp olive oil
2 medium onions, peeled and chopped
2 large cloves of garlic, crushed
2 sticks of celery, trimmed and sliced and/or a large carrot, peeled and chopped
$\frac{1}{2}$ a 400g can chopped tomatoes
1 litre vegetable stock made with 1 tbsp Marigold vegetable bouillon powder or an organic vegetable stock cube
2 medium courgettes (about 225g) trimmed and sliced into rounds
A handful of fresh green beans (about 125g) trimmed and quartered
410g can cannellini or borlotti beans
$\frac{1}{2}$ a small green cabbage trimmed and finely shredded or $\frac{1}{2}$ a bag of ready sliced greens or 3 tbsp chopped fresh parsley
2 tbsp red pesto
Salt and freshly ground black pepper
Freshly grated Parmesan to serve

Heat the olive oil in a large saucepan or casserole and cook the onion and garlic over a low heat for about 5 minutes. Add the chopped celery or carrots, cook for a few minutes more, then add the tomatoes and stock and bring to the boil. Lower the heat and simmer for about 10 minutes. Add the courgettes, green beans and cannellini beans (and half the cabbage, if using) and cook for another 30 minutes or until all the vegetables are soft, adding the remaining cabbage or parsley and pesto about 10 minutes before the end of the cooking time. Season to taste with salt and pepper and serve with grated Parmesan.

GUMBO Serves 4

 30 MINUTES – 1 HOUR

This mildly spiced vegetable stew is based on the Cajun dish gumbo which is normally made with seafood. But this veggie version is still good, rich and filling. Use fresh tomatoes rather than tinned ones when they're in season.

2 medium sized onions (about 100g each)
2 medium sized green peppers or 1 green and
   1 red pepper
2 medium sized courgettes (about 250g)
250g okra
4 tbsp cooking oil
2 sticks of celery
2 large cloves of garlic
1 tbsp tomato paste (optional)
2 level tsp sweet pimenton (Spanish paprika)
   or 1¹/₂ tsp ordinary paprika
1 level tsp allspice or mixed spice
1 level tbsp flour
4 medium to large fresh tomatoes, peeled and
   roughly chopped or half a 400g can of tinned
   tomatoes
1 litre of vegetable stock made with 1 tbsp
   Marigold vegan bouillon powder or an organic
   vegetable stock cube

200g frozen sweetcorn or a 326g can of
   sweetcorn, drained
2 handfuls of long grain rice (about 60g)
3 tbsp chopped parsley
Salt, plus lemon juice or vinegar to season
Hot pepper sauce (e.g. Tabasco) to serve

Peel and slice one of the onions. Quarter and de-seed the peppers then cut each quarter into two or three pieces. Cut the courgettes into chunks. Put all these vegetables in a baking tin with half the okra, trickle over 2 tbsp of the oil, toss the vegetables well in the oil and roast at 200C/ 400F/Gas 6 for about 40 minutes. About 15 minutes before their cooking time is up chop the other onion. Slice the celery and the remaining okra. Heat a large pan, add the remaining oil, tip in the onion and celery, cover and simmer for about 5-6 minutes until beginning to soften. Stir in the tomato paste if you're using fresh tomatoes that aren't very ripe, the pimenton or paprika, the allspice and the flour. Add the chopped tomatoes and sliced okra. Stir in the stock, bring to the boil and add the sweetcorn and rice. Cook briskly for 12-15 minutes until the rice is just cooked. Tip in the vegetables you've roasted and stir in the parsley. Check the seasoning, adding salt and a little lemon juice or vinegar to taste. Serve in deep bowls, with extra hot pepper sauce for those who like it!

When the weather warms up I don't stop eating soup – I just turn to Thai and other Asian recipes. Don't be afraid to serve them warm rather than piping hot.

THAI-STYLE SWEETCORN AND SPRING ONION CHOWDER Serves 2-3

PREPARATION AND COOKING TIME: 15-30 MINUTES

This is an odd but to my mind wholly successful integration of Thai flavours into an American chowder. Unless you're like my husband who likes neither sweetcorn nor coconut milk. Use fresh corn in season (July-September). It's cheap and has a really good flavour.

3 medium or 2 large whole corn on the cob or 200g frozen sweetcorn or a 326g can of sweetcorn, drained
1 bunch of spring onions or 1 medium onion, peeled and finely chopped
2 sticks of celery
2 tbsp sunflower or light olive oil
1 clove of garlic, crushed
1/4 tsp ground turmeric
2 mild fresh chillies, deseeded and finely sliced
1 medium potato, peeled and cut into small cubes
250ml vegetable stock made with 1 tsp Marigold vegetable bouillon powder
200ml coconut milk
1 tbsp lime or lemon juice
Salt to taste
3 tbsp chopped fresh coriander

Cut the base off each cob and peel off the husks. Propping it upright on its base, cut off the kernels, cutting downwards with a small sharp knife, then go over the cob with a small teaspoon scraping off the rest of the corn and the milky juices. Cut the top half of the leaves and the roots off the spring onions and chop the rest roughly. Clean the celery and chop it into rounds. Heat the oil in a large saucepan for a minute or two, then add the corn, onions, celery, crushed garlic and turmeric and chilli. Stir, cover the pan and cook on a low to moderate heat for 5-6 minutes. Add the diced potato and hot vegetable stock bring to the boil and simmer for about 20 minutes or until the vegetables are soft. Add the coconut milk and heat through then add the lime or lemon juice and season with salt to taste. Stir in the coriander and serve.

A LIGHT JAPANESEY KIND OF SOUP

Serves 2-3 PREPARATION AND COOKING TIME: UNDER 15 MINUTES

I've avoided putting tofu in the title of this recipe because I know some people run a mile from it. But give it a go. If you buy it from a health food shop you'll find it has a much better flavour and texture.

1 litre Easy All-Purpose Asian Broth
  (see following recipe)
1 tbsp light soy sauce (or 1-2 tsp dark soy sauce)
About 125g shitake, oyster or ordinary button
  mushrooms, wiped clean, trimmed and thinly
  sliced
A good handful of shredded greens (see footnote)
1 mild red chilli – or a hot one if you can take it –
  de-seeded and finely sliced
A good handful of well-rinsed beansprouts
  (about 110g)
50g firm tofu, cut into fine slices
2 tbsp chopped fresh coriander (optional)
Juice of $\frac{1}{2}$ a lime or a little rice wine vinegar

Heat up the broth until almost boiling and add the
soy sauce. Add the mushrooms, shredded greens
and chilli, bring back to the boil and simmer for a
couple of minutes. Add the beansprouts, tofu and
fresh coriander and cook for a couple of minutes
more. Adjust the seasoning to taste, adding a little
lime juice or rice vinegar and extra soy sauce to
taste if you think it needs it.

- You can buy packs of sliced greens but it's easy
  enough – and more effective for this kind of dish
  – to slice your own. Take an ordinary small dark
  green cabbage and peel off the outside leaves.
  Discard any really coarse ones and wash the
  rest thoroughly. Cut away the tough central
  rib of each leaf then roll up the rest of the leaf
  tightly and shred it finely with a sharp knife.

EASY, ALL-PURPOSE ASIAN BROTH
Serves 4 **UNDER 30 MINUTES**

*When you make anything like noodles or an
Asian-style soup you need a flavourful stock.
This makes enough for 4 servings but you can
keep it in the fridge for a couple of days.*

A handful of well-washed coriander stalks and
  roots
2 cloves of garlic
1 small (about 2 cm square) chunk of fresh ginger,
  peeled thickly sliced
1 tbsp Marigold vegan bouillon powder or a
  vegetable stock cube

Crush the stalks and the garlic with something
heavy – a rolling pin, the side of a (clean) bottle,
a can of beans... to help release the flavour.
Put them in a pan with the ginger. Dissolve the
bouillon powder or stock cube in a little hot water
then top up with 1 litre of cold water. Bring the
broth gradually to the boil then simmer very slowly
for about 20 minutes. Strain and discard the
flavourings.

Salads don't have to be raw. They can be just as refreshing based on cooked veg, as they are in Morocco or the Lebanon, and served warm rather than cold.

WARM BROAD BEAN AND MINT SALAD Serves 4
UNDER 15 MINUTES

500g frozen broad beans
1 medium onion, peeled and roughly chopped
3-4 tbsp olive oil
2 clove of garlic, peeled and crushed
1 level tsp ground cumin
Juice of half a lemon (about $1^1/_2$-2 tbsp)
2 tbsp each of finely chopped mint leaves and
    parsley or coriander leaves
Salt and freshly ground black pepper
Plain unsweetened yoghurt to serve (optional)
Feta cheese, to crumble over (optional)

Cook the beans in boiling salted water until just tender (about 4 minutes). Drain and set aside. Heat 2 tbsp of the oil in a small frying pan and fry the onion for about 4-5 minutes until soft. Add the garlic and cumin and cook for a minute then tip in the broad beans. Season to taste with salt, pepper and lemon juice and stir in the fresh herbs. Serve with the chickpea pancakes (opposite) or pitta bread and a good dollop of yoghurt or some Feta cheese.

CHICKPEA AND CUMIN PANCAKES

Serves 4 **15-30 MINUTES**

125g gram (chickpea) flour
$1^1/_2$ tsp baking powder
$1/_2$ tsp salt
$1/_4$ tsp chilli powder or cayenne pepper
$1^1/_2$ tsp cumin seeds or 1 rounded tsp ground cumin
1 fresh egg, lightly beaten
2 tbsp olive oi, plus extra for greasing the pan

Sift the chickpea flour, baking powder, salt and chilli powder into a large bowl. Sprinkle over the cumin seeds and make a hollow in the centre. Mix the egg in a jug with 150ml water and the olive oil and gradually add to the flour mixture, beating energetically to avoid lumps. Leave for 10 minutes then beat again. Heat a large non-stick frying pan and wipe it with a bit of scrunched up kitchen towel dipped in oil. Place tablespoons of the batter in the pan – you should probably be able to fit in four at a time. When the top of each pancake is covered with bubbles (about 20-30 seconds), flip it over with a spatula and cook the other side for a few seconds. Transfer to a warm plate while you cook the next batch of pancakes, stirring the mixture between each batch. You should have enough for 12 pancakes. Serve with the Warm Broad Bean and Mint Salad or GMVs (see p52).

• You can add some fresh coriander to the batter too if you're a coriander addict.

SPICED CARROT AND
BLACK OLIVE SALAD Serves 3-4

 15-30 MINUTES

This Moroccan-spiced salad works well alongside the Warm Broad Bean and Mint Salad (opposite). It tastes particularly good if you make it with new carrots when they come into the shops in the summer – the ones with the feathery, leafy tops.

350g new carrots
2 tbsp olive oil
$^1/_2$ tsp Moroccan spice mix (see p12)
A pinch of salt and sugar
75g pitted black olives marinated with herbs
A good squeeze of lemon
$^1/_2$ tsp roughly crushed roasted cumin seeds
   (see footnote below)
2 heaped tbsp chopped fresh coriander

Scrub the carrots and cut into thin diagonal slices. Heat the oil in a saucepan and cook the carrots gently for 3-4 minutes. Add the spices, salt and sugar and cook for a minute more. Add 2 tbsp water and put a lid on the pan. Cook until the carrots are soft, shaking the pan occasionally (about 15 minutes). Tip the carrots into a dish, cool, then mix in the olives and season with lemon juice. Sprinkle over the crushed cumin seeds and chopped coriander before serving.

• To roast cumin seeds put them in a small pan over a gentle heat and warm them through until they begin to change colour and smell fragrant.

MARINATED MUSHROOMS
WITH CORIANDER Serves 6

 UNDER 15 MINUTES (PLUS 2 HOURS MARINADING TIME)

A wonderful way of eating mushrooms. Not exactly a cooked salad but the effect of the marinade makes it taste like one. Good with raw spinach or other dark salad leaves.

2 tsp whole coriander seeds
$^1/_2$ tsp crushed chillies
2 tbsp Japanese seasoned rice vinegar
5 tbsp organic sunflower oil
Sea salt and freshly ground black pepper
375g pack sliced white mushrooms or 375g
   button mushrooms, wiped and sliced
2 rounded tbsp finely chopped fresh parsley

Crush the coriander seeds with a mortar and pestle or in a bowl with the end of a rolling pin. Place them in a large bowl with the crushed chillies, rice vinegar and sunflower oil and whisk together with a fork. Season to taste with salt and pepper. Tip the sliced mushrooms into the bowl, toss with the dressing and set aside for at least 2 hours. Just before serving mix in the chopped parsley.

Crunchiness is really appealing in a salad especially when most packet salads have no texture and taste at all. Lettuces to look for are iceberg, a good bet year round especially if you pair it with a tangy blue cheese dressing and Cos (or Sweet Romaine as it is rather pretentiously known nowadays) which has real flavour as well as crunch. Best value in high summer (June-September), use it to make a classic Caesar salad. Well, not so classic actually, given that it doesn't include anchovies but just as good....

ICEBERG LETTUCE WEDGES WITH BLUE CHEESE DRESSING Serves 4
15-30 MINUTES

Not the most slimming salad admittedly but it is tasty. Don't be tempted to whizz everything up together – the blue cheese will make it go a sickly blueish-green!

1 small to medium iceberg lettuce
For the dressing
2 tbsp white wine vinegar or cider vinegar
Salt, freshly ground black pepper
100ml light olive oil or sunflower or grapeseed oil
2 tbsp double or whipping cream
50g Danish Blue cheese
2 spring onions, trimmed and very finely sliced (optional)
Lemon juice to taste

Remove any soft or damaged outer leaves from the lettuce, cut off the base then cut the lettuce into four wedges. With a fork whisk the vinegar with a little salt and pepper then gradually whisk in the oil. Finally add the cream. Mash the blue cheese roughly and add to the dressing together with the spring onions. Set aside for 15-30 minutes, if you can, to let the flavours amalgamate. Check the seasoning, adding more salt and pepper if you think it needs it and a little squeeze of lemon juice if you have some. Put a lettuce wedge on each plate and spoon over the dressing.

• You could use the same dressing with halved Little Gem lettuces or with a pack of iceberg lettuce leaves. It also works well with a spinach and raw mushroom salad.

VEGGIE CAESAR SALAD Serves 4
UNDER 15 MINUTES

Warning: this salad could prove addictive.

A crisp, long-leaved lettuce (e.g. cos or Sweet Romaine)
1/2 a bunch of spring onions (about 3-4 onions) or a small handful of fresh chives
1/2 tsp Dijon mustard
Salt and freshly ground black pepper
1 rounded tbsp drained capers, roughly chopped
3-4 tbsp light olive or sunflower oil

3 tbsp grated fresh Parmesan
2 handfuls of crispy garlic croutons (see below)

Cut the base off the lettuce and remove any damaged outer leaves. Separate the leaves and dunk them in a big bowl of cold water. Shake them dry then dry in a (clean) kitchen towel or salad basket if you have one. Cut the base and top half of the green tops off the onions, slice them in quarters lengthways then chop them across into three. Whisk the mustard with a little salt and pepper and $1^1/_2$ tbsp of the pickling liquid from the caper jar then gradually whisk in 3 tbsp of the oil. Add the chopped capers, and a little more oil or pickling liquid if you think it needs it. Tear the lettuce leaves roughly with your hands into two or three pieces then put them in a big bowl with the sliced onions or chives. Pour over the dressing and mix with the leaves. Sprinkle over the Parmesan (if using), add half the croutons then toss again. Scatter over the remaining croutons and serve. It goes very well with hard boiled eggs.

• If you're short of time you could make this with a couple of bags of iceberg lettuce leaves.

CRISPY GARLIC CROUTONS
UNDER 15 MINUTES

This is the most brilliant way of producing really crisp garlic-flavoured croutons. You can also use them to sprinkle over a soup.

2 garlic-flavoured pitta breads
90ml (6 tbsp) light olive or sunflower oil

Cut the pitta breads into thinnish strips then across into squares. (Not too small otherwise it's a pain to turn them over when you fry them) Heat a large frying pan for 3-4 minutes then add the oil and heat another minute or so until really hot. Test the temperature by dropping a piece of pitta bread in the oil. It should sizzle but not burn. Tip the pitta squares in the oil, fry them for about 30 seconds then turn them over so that both sides are nice and brown. Remove them with a slotted spoon or a tablespoon and put them on a plate lined with kitchen paper to absorb any excess oil. Cool for 10 minutes before you use them.

SHOW-OFF

You don't need me to tell you that it's cheaper to eat in than eat out. You will almost certainly eat better too than in most of the places you can afford. It's also an opportunity to show off your new found skills. There will come a point when you'll find that there's nothing so rewarding – well almost nothing – as cooking for friends, whether it's a group of eight or just the one person you want to impress.

There will also come a moment when the whole thing threatens to spiral horribly out of control and you wish you'd never thought of the idea. Two solutions. Don't be too ambitious, attempting loads of dishes you've never tried before. And don't be too proud to accept offers of help whether they take the form of a bit of chopping or stirring, a salad or pud or (best of all) a hand with the washing-up....

It's also quite fun to theme the meal, which is what I've done over the following pages. Eat Italian. Try Thai. Go Greek – it's up to you.

If you don't want to have to worry whether your guests will enjoy the food, cook Italian: it's everyone's favourite. These are flashier, more time-consuming recipes than the ones you'll find elsewhere in the book, but are well worth the effort.

SPRING VEGETABLE RISOTTO (DAIRY-FREE)

Serves 6 as a starter, 3 as a main course

 15-30 MINUTES

Basing a risotto on spring vegetables like asparagus and peas is classic. Leaving out butter and Parmesan isn't but surprisingly the end result still tastes deliciously creamy.

A 250g bunch of asparagus
4 tbsp olive oil (ideally extra virgin)
1 small to medium onion, peeled and finely chopped
250g risotto rice (e.g. arborio or carnaroli)
1 litre hot vegetable stock made with 1 rounded tbsp Marigold vegan bouillon powder or an organic vegetable stock cube
A small (125ml) glass of dry white wine
125g podded fresh or frozen peas
2 heaped tbsp chopped dill leaves or parsley
Salt, pepper and lemon juice to taste

Cut the tips off the asparagus spears about 7cm down the stalk. Cut off any woody bits at the base then peel each spear thinly with a vegetable peeler, and chop them into small pieces. Heat 3 tbsp of the olive oil in a non-stick saucepan and add the onion. Stir and cook over a moderate heat for about 3 minutes then tip in the rice and stir. Let it cook for about 3 minutes without colouring, stirring occasionally so it doesn't catch on the pan. Meanwhile heat the stock in another saucepan till it's almost boiling and leave on a low heat. Pour the wine into the rice – it will sizzle and evaporate almost immediately. Add the chopped asparagus stalks and the fresh or frozen peas then start to add the stock bit by bit, about half a mugful at a time, stirring the risotto in between. Cook it until the liquid has almost been absorbed. Then add the next lot of stock and repeat until all the stock is used up and the rice is creamy but still has a little 'bite' to it (i.e. you don't want it soft and mushy). This will take about 20 minutes. While you're stirring away cook the asparagus tips for about 4 minutes in the hot stock then scoop them out and set them aside on a plate or a saucer. When the risotto is cooked stir in the dill and season with salt, pepper and a good squeeze of lemon juice (about 2-3 tsp). Pour the remaining oil into the saucepan you used to heat the stock and gently reheat the asparagus tips. Serve the risotto in small bowls with one or two asparagus tips on top.

SPICED BUTTERNUT SQUASH RISOTTO WITH CRISPY SAGE

Serves 6 as a starter, 3 as a main course
15-30 MINUTES

This is a fantastic recipe I saw Jamie Oliver demonstrate at the Good Food Show last year.

1 medium or ½ a large butternut squash (about 1kg)
8 tbsp sunflower or light olive oil
1 rounded tbsp coriander seeds
1 level tsp crushed chillies or 2 dried red chillies, deseeded and finely chopped or a little chilli sauce
1 medium onion
A good lump of butter (about 20g)
1 litre hot stock made with 1 tbsp Marigold vegetable bouillon powder
A pinch of saffron or ¼ tsp turmeric
1 large clove of garlic
250g risotto rice
 A small glass of white wine (about 125ml)
2 tbsp freshly grated Parmesan
Salt and pepper
A small pack (about 20g) sage leaves

Wipe the squash clean and cut it lengthways into quarters – or, if using half a squash, in half. (The skin is tough – you'll need a large sharp knife.) Scoop out the seeds then cut each piece across into 4 or 5 big chunks. Cut the skin off each chunk (easiest if you lay each piece on a chopping board and slice downwards) and cut them in half. Preheat your oven to 190C/375F/Gas 5. Pour 3 tbsp of the oil into a roasting dish. Crush the coriander seeds and chillies. Turn the chunks of squash in the oil and sprinkle with the crushed spices. Roast for about 40 minutes until soft, turning them over half the way through. Meanwhile start the risotto. Peel and finely chop the onion. Heat a heavy pan on the hob, add 2 tbsp of oil then add the butter. Cook on a low heat till the onion is soft, stirring occasionally (about 3-4 minutes). Make your stock and keep it hot (either in a small pan or by popping it into the microwave when it cools down). Put the saffron (if using) in a cup and pour over 1 tbsp of the warm stock. Leave to infuse. Once the onion is soft add the crushed garlic, turmeric and saffron, stir then turn the heat up slightly and tip in the rice. Cook it for about three minutes stirring continually so it doesn't catch on the bottom of the pan. Pour in the wine and when the sizzling has died down and it has evaporated add about half a mugful of hot stock. Stir until the stock has been absorbed then add more stock and repeat until the rice is creamy but still has some 'bite' and the stock has all been absorbed. Turn off the heat. Take the squash out of the oven. Roughly mash half of it and break up the other half into chunks. Stir it into the risotto along with the cheese. Add salt and pepper to taste. Cover and set the pan aside. Wipe the pan in which you heated the stock and cover the base with a thin layer of oil. Heat for about 3-4 minutes. Strip the sage leaves off their stalks and drop them into the pan, they should rise up and crisp in a couple of seconds. Scoop them out with a slotted spoon and drain them on kitchen paper. Serve on warm plates with the sage leaves sprinkled on top.

ROAST VEGETABLE LASAGNE

Serves 4-6 **OVER 1 HOUR**

There's no point in pretending this isn't a complicated recipe. There are far easier ways of combining pasta and roast veggies (see p82) but I know people are crazy about lasagne and it's cheap so here we go. You can try making it without pre-cooking the lasagne but I always find it goes slightly cardboardy and makes the finished dish dry.

1 large aubergine (about 350g)
Sea salt and freshley ground pepper
3 peppers (a mixture of red and green)
125ml olive oil
2 medium to large courgettes (about 300g)
2 cloves of garlic
2 x 400g cans of tomatoes
250g pack dried green lasagne
150g freshly grated Parmesan or 200g grated
　vegetarian Cheddar

First prepare the vegetables. Rinse the aubergine, cut off the stalk and slice it into medium-thick slices (about the thickness of a pound coin). Lay them out on a chopping board or clean work surface, sprinkle them both sides with salt and leave them for 30 minutes to get rid of the bitter juices. Meanwhile set the oven to 200C/400F/Gas 6. Rinse the peppers, cut them into quarters and cut away the stalks, white pith and seeds.

Lay them out on a baking tray and trickle a little olive oil over both sides. Roast them for about 40 minutes or until just soft then cut each quarter into two. Once the aubergines have little beads of moisture all over them transfer them to a colander or sieve, rinse them thoroughly under the cold tap to get rid of the salt and pat them dry with kitchen towel. Lay them out on another baking sheet, trickle oil over both sides, rubbing it in well and roast them for about 25 minutes. (If you only have one baking sheet, cook the peppers first then cook the aubergines). After roasting, lower the oven temperature to 190C/375F/Gas 5 ready to bake the lasagne. Rinse the courgettes, cut off the stalks and cut them into diagonal slices about the same thickness as the aubergines. Heat about 3 tbsp of olive oil in a frying pan and fry them quickly on both sides until they begin to brown. (You will need to do this in two or three batches.) Set aside the cooked courgettes on a plate, turn the heat down and add the crushed garlic to the pan. Stir for a few seconds then tip in the tinned tomatoes and break them up with a spatula or wooden spoon. Simmer for a few minutes then season with salt and pepper. Finally (told you this was time-consuming) bring a large pan of water to the boil. Add a little salt and a tablespoon of oil and drop in the lasagne sheets one by one. Cook for 4-8 minutes depending on how thick your lasagne is (cheap lasagne is usually thicker) until no longer hard, drain and rinse with cold water. Now you can assemble the lasagne.

You need a deep, ideally rectangular, dish slightly smaller than the average roasting tin. Grease it with a little olive oil then put a couple of spoonfuls of the tomato sauce over the bottom. Lay a layer of roast veggies over the top, season lightly with salt and pepper, spoon over some more sauce (about $1/4$ to a $1/3$ of what you have left in the pan) and sprinkle over about 2 heaped tbsp of grated Parmesan or Cheddar. Lay over another layer of lasagne sheets, then another layer of vegetables, sauce and cheese, ending with a layer of lasagne. (Depending on the size of your dish you may be able to make a third layer but leave enough tomato sauce to top the lasagne.) Finally spoon the remaining sauce over the lasagne and top with a good layer of grated cheese. At this point you can refrigerate the lasagne and cook it later or even the following day, bringing it to room temperature again before you cook it. Trickle a little extra olive oil over the top of the lasagne and bake for about 40-45 minutes until nicely browned and bubbling. Serve with plenty of crusty bread and a big green salad.

ANTIPASTI

Grilled or roasted vegetables also make a colourful first course or antipasto drizzled with olive oil and and sprinkled with fresh basil leaves (see GMVs p52). Serve with some ciabatta, focaccia or simple country bread. Alternatively you could buy them ready-grilled or roasted from an Italian deli (usually cheaper than buying jars). The Marinated Mushrooms with Coriander on p107 would also be good or this easy and delicious salad below.

MOZZARELLA AND TOMATO SALAD
Serves 4-6 **UNDER 15 MINUTES**

2 x 125g balls of authentic Italian Mozzarella
About 450g ripe cherry tomatoes
3 x the Italian-Style Oil, Lemon and Parsley Salad
   on p55 (minus the garlic)

Cut or tear the Mozzarella into small chunks. Halve or quarter the tomatoes. Mix the two together in a bowl with the dressing. That's it!

• You could leave out the parsley and use a handful of torn, fresh basil leaves instead.

I don't know why but the Italians have a brilliant line in boozy desserts – maybe because they don't have a tradition of elaborate patisserie like the French. Here are two deliciously indulgent examples.

STRAWBERRY TIRAMISU TART

Serves 4-6 **UNDER 1 HOUR**

Ready-rolled pastry has put flashy tarts within reach of even the most incompetent cook but pack sizes vary significantly. The ideal one to use for this is Sara Lee's which is nice and thin – if you use a bigger pack, cut off the amount you need and roll it out a little more thinly. The other thing that really helps is a hand-held electric whisk – if you don't have one try and borrow one.

230g pack of ready-rolled puff pastry (e.g. Sarah Lee)
2 large eggs, separated (see p65)
2 level tbsp caster sugar plus 1 tsp for sprinkling
   on the pastry
250g Mascarpone (from an Italian deli if possible)
2-3 tbsp white rum
400g ripe, thickly sliced strawberries (if not very
   ripe see below)

You will need a large, lightly oiled square baking sheet. Preheat the oven to 200C/400F/Gas 6. Take the pastry out of the fridge and let it rest for 10 minutes before you use it. Unroll it carefully onto the baking sheet, removing the greaseproof paper. If it overhangs your baking tray cut a thin strip from round the edge of the pastry. Lightly whisk one of the egg whites with a fork until frothy and brush a thin layer onto the pastry. Sprinkle with 1 tsp of sugar then prick the base all over with the prongs of a fork and bake for 10-12 minutes until puffy and brown. Leave on one side to cool while you make the topping. Tip the Mascarpone into a bowl and gradually work in the rum with a wooden spoon, then beat it until the mixture is completely smooth. Whisk the egg yolks with the remaining caster sugar until pale, thick and creamy. Gently fold the Mascarpone into the eggs and mix until thoroughly blended. When the pastry base is cool transfer it to a large serving plate or tray and spread over the creamed Mascarpone with a spatula, taking it almost up to the edges. Arrange the strawberries over the top and chill until ready to serve.

WARNING
THIS DESSERT CONTAINS UNCOOKED EGGS SO SHOULD BE AVOIDED BY PREGNANT WOMEN.

• If the strawberries you're using seem a bit sharp, slice them, put them in a bowl and sprinkle them with about 1 tbsp of caster sugar. Give them a stir and leave them for 20-30 minutes before you use them to top the tart.
• When strawberries are out of season you could make this with a mixture of white and red grapes, substituting the Italian lemon liqueur Limoncello for the white rum.

PEACHES IN PROSECCO

Serves 6 **OVER 1 HOUR**
(INCLUDING TIME IN FRIDGE)

I hesitated about putting this in because it's not cheap but it's so delicious, so easy and looks so fab that I thought it justified blowing the budget. You only want to make it in summer though when you have really, really ripe (and cheap) peaches.

4 large perfectly ripe (ready to eat) white peaches
  or nectarines
1 tbsp freshly squeezed lemon juice
200ml own-label peach schnapps (like Archers)
1 x 750ml bottle of chilled prosecco (Italian
  sparkling wine) or Cava (see footnote)
125g ripe raspberries

Halve the peaches by cutting vertically round the outside of the fruit with a sharp knife and twisting the two halves in opposite directions. Halve each half again and peel away the skin (unless using nectarines) then cut each piece into three slices. Put the peach pieces in a bowl and gently mix them with the lemon juice to stop them discolouring, then pour over the peach schnapps and about two thirds of the chilled prosecco. Cover the bowl with cling-film and place in the fridge for an hour or so for the flavours to amalgamate. Keep the rest of the prosecco in the fridge too. Check before serving to see if it's sweet enough for you: if not add an extra splash of peach schnapps. To serve arrange the peach slices in individual glasses or glass bowls, layering them up with a few raspberries. Ladle the peach schnapps and prosecco over the fruit then top up with more prosecco if necessary to cover the fruit.

• You may be aware that not all wine is vegetarian or vegan – some producers use animal-derived products such as gelatine and egg whites for fining (clarifying) their wines. Most organic wines don't, so it's worth looking out for them in health food shops and independent wine merchants along with wines that are labelled 'unfined'. Many of the wines now stocked by supermarkets are now suitable for vegetarians and vegans.

• See also Sweet Wine with Dipping Biscuits and Affogato (both on p139).

Eating Greek (or anywhere else in the Eastern Mediterrean) is a rewarding experience for the aspiring veggie gourmet. A selection of mezedes (or mezze, as they're called elsewhere in the Middle East) makes quite a feast in itself, especially for vegans. The pie or potato bake on the following pages will always go down well. Round off with one of the fabulously fruity puds.

EASY ROAST RED PEPPER HUMMUS Serves 8

 UNDER 15 MINUTES

Red pepper hummus has become very popular, but it's not cheap. Here's a version that will easily serve 8. Only drawback – you need a blender.

A 400g can of hummus, drained
A small jar of roasted red peppers or 1¹/₂-2 medium red peppers, roasted and cooled (see p82)
¹/₂ tsp sweet pimenton or paprika or ¹/₄ tsp chilli powder
1 tbsp olive oil
Salt, pepper and lemon juice to taste

Drain any liquid away from the hummus and tip it into a deep bowl or the bowl of a food processor or blender. Drain the red peppers, slice roughly and add to the hummus along with the olive oil then whizz until smooth. Season to taste with pimenton, salt, pepper and lemon juice. Serve with pitta bread.

• This also makes a good dip for raw veg or a good dressing for grilled veg (see GMVs p52).

CHARRED AUBERGINE AND TOMATO SALAD Serves 4-6, depending on how many other dishes you're serving

 30 MINUTES – 1 HOUR

There's a hugely popular Greek dip which involves charring or roasting an aubergine then gouging out the flesh and making a dip. I've never been really grabbed by it because a) it takes ages to make b) turns a dirty beige colour and c) you discard the skin which is the best bit. Here's the solution – a salad which includes all those lovely smoky flavours.

2 medium or 1 large aubergine (about 500g)
4 tbsp olive oil
1 medium onion (about 100g), peeled and roughly chopped
1 clove of garlic, peeled and crushed
2 medium tomatoes, skinned, de-seeded and diced (see p41)
2 tbsp roughly chopped parsley and 1 tbsp chopped mint leaves
1-1¹/₂ tbsp lemon juice
1 tsp ground cumin
Salt and pepper

Cut the stalks off each aubergine, cut in half lengthways then cut into cubes. Heat a wok for about 2 minutes over a high heat, add the oil, heat for a few seconds then tip in the aubergine cubes. Stir-fry over a moderate heat for about 5 minutes until lightly browned then turn the heat down low, add the onion and garlic, stir, cover the pan and cook gently for a further 15 minutes, stirring from time to time. Tip the aubergine into a shallow dish while you prepare the other ingredients. When the aubergine is cool (about 20 minutes), cut it up roughly with a knife and fork, then mix in the chopped tomato, parsley and mint. Season with the lemon juice, cumin and salt and pepper. Serve with pitta bread.

- You could replace the parsley and mint with fresh coriander.
- The salad will also go well with some Feta cheese and olives.

GREEK SALAD SALSA

Serves 6-8 **UNDER 15 MINUTES**

I don't know why but chopping the traditional Greek salad up small makes it taste more delicious. It also makes it more like a salsa. It would also go really well with felafel or a veggie burger.

500g cherry tomatoes
A large cucumber (about 600g)
200g Feta cheese
150g pitted dry black olives
1 medium red onion, peeled and roughly chopped
4 tbsp lemon juice
125ml extra virgin olive oil
2 tsp dried oregano
Freshly ground black pepper

Cut the tomatoes into 4 or 8 pieces, depending on size. Quarter the cucumber, cut away the seeds and cut into small dice the same size as the tomato pieces. Cut the cheese into similar sized small cubes and the olives into quarters and add to the tomato and cucumber along with the chopped onion. Pour over the lemon juice and olive oil, season with the oregano and black pepper and toss together carefully so as not to break up the cheese too much. Serve with warm pitta bread or (less traditionally) couscous.

- Although I often advocate substituting a white crumbly English cheese for Feta for this dish you do need the real thing. If you have a Greek or Cypriot grocer near you – or even a health food shop you'll probably find it cheaper there than in the supermarket.

The Greeks have some truly fabulous pies, often served lukewarm which seems to bring out their flavour. Once you get the hang of handling pastry – which isn't hard – they're a doddle.

GREEK SPINACH, LEEK AND FETA PIE

Serves 6 **OVER 1 HOUR**

Traditionally this would have been made with filo rather than puff pastry but puff pastry is cheaper, less fiddly and more filling.

2 medium leeks or 1 large leek (about 250g)
   or a bunch of spring onions
25g butter
750g frozen leaf spinach, thawed
300g Feta cheese
2 tbsp chopped mint leaves or dill or 2 tsp dried
   mint or dried dill
Juice of $1/2$ a lemon
2 eggs, lightly beaten
Salt, pepper and a little nutmeg if you have some
500g chilled puff pastry

You will need a rectangular baking tray (about 27 x 37 cm). Clean and slice the leeks as described on p58. Place a pan over a low heat, add the butter and stir in the leeks. Cover and cook for about 6-7 minutes until soft. Take handfuls of the spinach and squeeze hard to extract all the water then place in a large bowl and chop roughly. Chop the Feta into small cubes and add to the spinach together with the leeks and the mint or dill.
Add $2/3$ of the beaten egg, the lemon juice, a little salt and quite a bit of pepper. Cut the pastry in two, making one half slightly bigger than the other, sprinkle some flour on your (presumably clean) work surface and roll out the smaller half thinly. Using a knife, trim the edges straight and lay it on a lightly greased baking tray. Heat the oven to 220C/425F/Gas 7. Spoon the filling onto the pastry leaving a small border round the edges. Roll out the other half of the pastry so it is slightly bigger than the base. Brush or smear the exposed edges of the base with a little beaten egg, then carefully lower the top piece of pastry over the filling without stretching it and press the edges together. Trim off the overlapping pastry with a knife, then turning your knife round to the blunt side drag the edges in at regular intervals round the edge of the pie to hold them together. Cut three vertical slits in the top of the pie and brush with the remaining beaten egg. Place the pie in the oven and cook for 20 minutes then lower the heat to 200C/400F/Gas 6 and cook for another 15-20 minutes until the pastry is well risen and brown. Serve hot or lukewarm with a salad.

- If you feel nervous about rolling out pastry you could buy 2 x 375g packs of ready-rolled pastry and roll one piece out to make it a bit larger than the other. More expensive but less hassle.
- You can make the pie ahead and put it in the fridge but allow about 10 minutes extra cooking time.

GREEK-STYLE POTATO, COURGETTE AND FETA BAKE

Serves 4 **OVER 1 HOUR**

This is one of my favourite new dishes.
You may have to end up doubling the quantity
or making two it's so good.

Half a bunch of spring onions (about 4)
4 medium sized potatoes (about 600g), peeled
2 medium to large courgettes (about 275g-300g)
4 sprigs of mint
2 tbsp olive oil
200g Feta cheese
Freshly ground black pepper
300ml vegetable stock made with 1 rounded tsp
   vegetable bouillon powder or $1/2$ a vegetable
   stock cube

Preheat the oven to 190C/375F/Gas 5. Trim the roots and the top half of the green leaves off the spring onions. Cut them lengthways into quarters then across into three. Halve and finely slice the potatoes. Cut the ends off each courgette and slice the rest finely. Pull the leaves off the mint and chop roughly. Pour 1tbsp of the olive oil into a large baking dish and smear it round the base and sides of the dish. Put a layer of potatoes over the bottom of the dish (about one third of the sliced potato), top with half the onions, half the sliced courgettes and half the Feta, evenly crumbled over the courgettes. Scatter over half the mint and season with freshly ground black pepper. Repeat with another layer of potato, onion, courgette, Feta and mint then finish with a layer of potato.
Pour the stock over the vegetables then trickle the remaining olive oil over the top of the dish. Bake for an hour to an hour and a quarter or until the potatoes are completely tender (see footnote) and the top is brown and crispy. (About half way through the cooking time tilt the pan and spoon the juices over the potatoes.) Once cooked allow the bake to cool for 10 minutes if you can bear to, then serve with a tomato salad (sliced tomatoes dressed with a little oil and vinegar).

• To tell if the potatoes are done stick the point of a knife through the bake. If it meets with any resistance give it another 10 minutes or so.

The Greeks, like other populations in the Eastern Mediterranean have a fondness for sticky, syrup-drenched nut pastries like baklava and you can easily solve the problem of pud by buying some of those. Much nicer I think though is to base your dessert on fruit, Greek yoghurt and honey – and a little sweet wine if you can run to it.

ROAST NECTARINES WITH GREEK YOGHURT AND HONEY Serves 4

15-30 MINUTES

Fruit like nectarines, peaches and plums are rarely ripe here but roast them and they'll taste deliciously sweet.

10-12 medium sized yellow-fleshed nectarines
  or peaches
50g butter
2 tbsp unrefined caster sugar mixed with 1 tsp
  ground cinnamon
1 large (500g) carton Greek yoghurt
Some good, preferably Greek, runny honey

Run a knife vertically round the outside of each nectarine, cutting through to the stone. Holding one half of the nectarine in each hand, twist them in different directions to pull them apart. Cut out the stone if it hasn't come away. Pre-heat your oven to 220C/425F/Gas 7. Place the nectarines, cut side upwards in a lightly oiled roasting tin, put a small chunk of butter in each half, sprinkle with the sugar and cinnamon and roast them for 15 minutes. Serve with dollops of Greek yoghurt and honey drizzled over the top.

- You can also make this with peaches, apricots or plums.
- If you're having a barbecue you could cook the nectarines on that (having cleaned the grilling rack up a bit first so you don't get bits of veggie burger on them). Melt the butter gently in a small saucepan or microwave and brush or smear it over the nectarine halves. Lightly oil a rack and lay the nectarines over it, cut side downwards. Barbecue for about 15 minutes (depending how hot your barbecue is), turning them half way through the cooking time and sprinkling the cinnamon sugar over them.

GRAPE COMPOTE WITH MUSCAT WINE AND HONEY

Serves 6 **15-30 MINUTES**
(PLUS COOKING AND CHILLING TIME)

This easy and delicious way of cooking grapes is typically Greek – very sweet but perfectly offset by the slight sharpness and creaminess of the yoghurt. It seems to benefit from 24 hours in the fridge so make it the day before if you're sufficiently well organised.

1 large bunch (about 600g/1lb 5 oz) red seedless
  grapes

250ml muscat dessert wine
3 level tbsp Greek honey or other runny honey
1 tsp vanilla essence (optional but good)
2 pieces of star anise (optional)
1 stick of cinnamon
1 large (500g) tub of creamy Greek-style yoghurt

Pick the grapes off the stalks and rinse. Put the wine, honey, vanilla essence, cinnamon stick and star anise in a saucepan over a very low heat and warm it until the honey has liquified. Bring the syrup to the boil and simmer for a couple of minutes. Tip in the grapes, bring back to the boil and simmer for 2 minutes, shaking the pan occasionally to ensure the grapes cook evenly. Remove the grapes with a slotted spoon and then boil the remaining syrup briskly until reduced by half (about 10 minutes). Set aside to cool for 10 minutes then strain the syrup over the grapes. When the compote is completely cold chill it for at least 3-4 hours in the fridge. Serve in a shallow dish with a bowl of stirred creamy yoghurt alongside.

SLICED ORANGES WITH METAXA

Serves 6 Ve 15-30 MINUTES
(PLUS COOLING AND CHILLING TIME)

A good option if you fancy making a Greek meal in the winter. Metaxa, often referred to as Greek 'brandy', is a mixture of brandy and muscat wine infused with rose petals and herbs. It comes in several grades – 3 star, 5 star and 7 star. Buy the best you can afford.

250g caster sugar
6 medium sized oranges
3-4 tbsp of Metaxa
Lemon juice to taste

Put the sugar in a saucepan with 250ml water and place it over a low heat, stirring occasionally until all the sugar crystals have dissolved and the liquid is completely clear. Bring up to the boil and boil without stirring for 3-4 minutes then turn off the heat and leave to cool. With a sharp knife score through the skin of the oranges, dividing them into quarters but without cutting through the orange itself. Put in a large bowl and pour over a kettle full of boiling water. Leave for a minute then drain the water away and cover the oranges with cold water. Peel the oranges, removing as much of the white pith as possible. Slice the oranges across into rounds, discarding any pips but carefully preserving the juice, then lay the orange slices in a bowl. Mix the Metaxa with the syrup and taste, adding a squeeze of lemon juice if it's too sweet. Pour over the oranges and chill.

• See note on p13 about vegetarian wines.

If you haven't already encountered the zesty, invigorating flavours of Thai food you're in for a treat. It's one of the most exciting and varied cuisines for vegetarians and vegans (though you do have to be careful about the shrimp paste and fish sauce in some shop-bought sauces). Thais would serve a number of dishes on the table at the same time – say, a fried dish, a curry, a salad, a noodle dish and rice but unless you're an experienced cook or have plenty of willing helpers I'd stick to one or two. Prepare to be seduced...

THAI CHICKPEA AND CASHEW NUT CAKES Serves 6 -8

(though 4 could easily make short work of them)

 OVER 1 HOUR

A veggie equivalent of the ever-popular Thai fish cakes. Not difficult but it does involve a fair amount of chopping so rope in someone to help.

100g broken cashew nuts
1 large carrot (about 125g) peeled and roughly chopped
1 400g can of chickpeas, drained and rinsed
1/2 a bunch of spring onions, trimmed and very finely sliced or a small onion, peeled and very finely chopped
3 lime leaves finely shredded or the grated zest of a fresh lime
Juice of half a lime
3 heaped tbsp finely chopped fresh coriander leaves
1-2 tbsp vegetarian red Thai curry paste (depending how hot the paste is)
1 fresh green chilli, de-seeded and finely chopped (optional)
2 cloves of garlic, peeled and finely chopped (optional)
1 medium egg, lightly beaten
25g gram flour or plain flour, plus extra flour for dusting
150ml vegetable oil for frying

Finely chop the nuts, carrot and chickpeas in a food processor or using the chopping attachment of a hand-held blender. (If you use the latter you may have to do each of them separately.) Don't make it too smooth – you want some texture. Tip into a large bowl and add the sliced or chopped onion, lime leaves or lime zest, lime juice, fresh coriander and curry paste plus extra garlic and chilli if you think it needs it. Stir in the flour and beaten egg. Scoop out tablespoons of the mixture and form them into little cakes about 5-6 cm in diameter. (You'll find this easiest with wet hands.) Dust them with flour and lay them on a baking tray then refrigerate them for at least an hour. Pour about 150ml of oil into a wok and heat for about 4 minutes until hot enough to make a cube of bread sizzle when you chuck it in. Carefully lower about half the patties into the pan, fry for about a minute then turn them over and fry the other side – about 2-3 minutes in total until they're brown and crispy. Drain on sheets of paper towel and serve immediately with a Thai salad or dipping sauce.

THAI-STYLE DIPPING SAUCE

Serves 4-6 **UNDER 15 MINUTES**

5 tbsp sweet chilli sauce
2-3 tbsp lime or lemon juice
2 tbsp water
1-2 tsp light soy sauce
$1/3$ of a cucumber, peeled, seeded and chopped
   into fine dice
2 tbsp finely chopped fresh coriander leaves

Mix the chilli sauce with the lime or lemon juice and water. Season to taste with soy sauce and stir in the cucumber and chopped coriander.

THAI GREEN APPLE SALAD

Serves 4, or 6 with other dishes

 15-30 MINUTES

Believe me, this is very, very good.

50g shelled, roasted, unsalted peanuts (see footnote)
1 tsp sunflower or light olive oil
Juice of 1 large lemon (about 3 tbsp)
2 medium to large Granny Smith apples (about
   325-350g)
1 large carrot (about 150g)
2 spring onions, trimmed and finely sliced
1 clove of garlic, peeled and crushed
1 mild green or red chilli, de-seeded and finely
   chopped

2 tbsp light soy sauce
2 tsp caster sugar
$1/2$ tsp Thai chilli jam (optional)
4-5 mint leaves, very finely chopped
2 tbsp chopped fresh coriander leaves
Salt or extra lemon juice to taste

Prepare the peanuts as described below (also see footnote). Put the lemon juice in a bowl. Quarter the apples and chop into short, thin strips, mixing them with the lemon juice as you go so that they don't brown. Peel and cut the carrot into similar sized strips and add to the apple along with the sliced spring onions, crushed garlic and chopped chilli. Mix the soy sauce with the sugar (and chilli jam, if using) and pour over the salad. Chop the peanuts roughly and add to the salad with the mint and coriander leaves. Check the seasoning, adding more lemon juice and/or a little salt if you think it needs it.

WARNING

NEVER SERVE PEANUTS OR OTHER NUTS TO ANYONE WITHOUT CHECKING WHETHER THEY'RE ALLERGIC TO THEM.

• For this and other peanut recipes buy whole roasted peanuts in the shell (monkey nuts!). Just shell them, rub off their skins and chop them. Otherwise, buy a bag of unsalted, shelled peanuts. Put the amount you need into a small pan without any oil and heat gently, shaking the pan occasionally until they start to brown. Remove the pan from the heat, cool, then tip them onto a clean tea-towel and rub off the skins.

I have to admit I'm not a great one for making Thai curries from scratch. If you fiddle around with ready-made curry sauces you can make a perfectly good one. Take care though that you get one that's suitable for vegetarians. Some contain shrimp paste and fish sauce.

THAI RED VEGETABLE CURRY

15-30 MINUTES

How hot you make this is up to you and depends on the sauce you use. Most mainstream brands are comparatively mild but if you find them too fiery add a little coconut milk. If you want it hotter add an extra chilli or a little red chilli paste, chilli jam or a few drops of hot pepper sauce. But only a little at a time, tasting it carefully after each addition! Remember people's tolerance to chilli varies considerably particularly if they're not familiar with Thai food.

1 large aubergine (about 350g), cut into even-sized cubes
Salt
125g sugarsnap peas
100g fine green beans, trimmed and cut into two
3 tbsp cooking oil
1/2 bunch of spring onions, trimmed and cut into fine slices
1 red pepper, quartered, de-seeded and cut into squares
2 large cloves of garlic, peeled and crushed

A small chunk of ginger, peeled and grated (optional)
3 lime leaves or dried lime leaves soaked in warm water (optional)
1 large jar or sachet of Thai red curry sauce (about 450-500g)
Juice of 1 lime or 2 tbsp lemon juice
A handful of torn basil leaves (Thai basil if you can get it) or 3 heaped tbsp chopped fresh coriander

If you have time sprinkle the aubergine generously with salt and leave to drain in a colander for 30 minutes. Bring a pan of water to the boil, tip in the sugarsnap peas and green beans, bring back to the boil, cook for a minute then drain and rinse the vegetables under cold running water. Rinse the aubergine thoroughly and pat dry with kitchen paper. Heat a wok or large frying pan, add the oil and fry the aubergine, stirring occasionally for about 5-6 minutes until beginning to brown. Add the spring onions and red pepper then stir-fry for another 3-4 minutes. Add the crushed garlic, grated ginger and lime leaves if using, then add the beans and sugarsnap peas and tip in the red curry sauce and the lime or lemon juice. Stir well, turn the heat down, cover the pan and leave to simmer for 10-15 minutes. Check the seasoning adding more lemon and a little salt if you think it needs it. Just before serving stir in the basil.

• See also the Thai Tofu, Sweetcorn and Sugarsnap Pea Curry in *Beyond Baked Beans*.

VEGGIE PAD THAI

Serves 4, or 6 with other dishes
15-30 MINUTES

Pad Thai is one of Thailand's most famous noodle dishes – normally made with seafood but this veggie version works really well. Treat it like a stir-fry and get all your ingredients prepared beforehand. The actual cooking only takes a few minutes.

200g medium rice noodles
3 tbsp sunflower oil or other light cooking oil
Half a bunch of spring onions, peeled and finely sliced
A small (300g) pack Chinese beansprout stir-fry
150g pack golden marinated tofu
2 large cloves of garlic, peeled and crushed
Juice of 1 lime plus 1 whole lime
1 tbsp light soy sauce
1 tbsp sweet chilli sauce
75g shelled, unsalted, roast peanuts (see p125), roughly chopped
2-3 tsp of sesame oil
3 heaped tbsp chopped coriander, plus a few extra coriander leaves for decoration

Drop the noodles into a large pan of boiling water with a little oil added, bring back to the boil, boil for a minute then drain and rinse under cold running water. Heat a wok or large frying pan add the oil then tip in the spring onions and beansprouts and stir-fry for a couple of minutes. Add the tofu and cook for a further minute then add the crushed garlic, lime juice, soy sauce and chilli sauce. Stir, then turn the heat right down and tip in the noodles. Using a serving spoon and fork toss them with the rest of the ingredients till they are thoroughly mixed together. Add the chopped peanuts, sesame oil and coriander and toss again, then serve in warm bowls with a few extra coriander leaves sprinkled on top. Serve with a lime wedge on the side and put out the soy sauce, sesame oil and sweet chilli sauce so everyone can add more if they wish.

WARNING
NEVER SERVE PEANUTS OR OTHER NUTS TO ANYONE WITHOUT CHECKING WHETHER THEY'RE ALLERGIC TO THEM.

The Thais have a delightfully playful attitude to desserts which are generally very sweet and brightly coloured. These aren't authentic but they are definitely in the spirit of the ones I came across in Bangkok.

PINK COCONUT RICE

Serves 6

 **30 MINUTES TO 1 HOUR (PLUS COOLING TIME)**

Your friends won't believe that something so wickedly creamy contains not a drop of milk or cream. You don't have to add the pink colouring if you find it too kitsch but I love it – particularly with the brilliant orange of the mango salad with which it goes perfectly.

4 tbsp (55g) dessert or pudding rice
A 400ml can of coconut milk
10 cardamom pods
75g (5 tbsp) unrefined caster sugar
A few drops of pink food colour (from the baking section of your supermarket).

Put the rice in a non-stick saucepan. Measure the coconut milk into a measuring jug then add water to come to the 600ml mark. Stir and pour over the rice. Lightly crush the cardamom pods and add them to the pan. Bring gradually to the boil, giving the contents an occasional stir then turn the heat right down and simmer for about 40-45 minutes,

stirring from time to time to make sure it doesn't stick. Take off the heat and stir in the sugar and couple of drops of pink colouring and leave to cool. Pick out the crushed cardamoms with a teaspoon then refrigerate until ready to eat. Serve in glass dishes with the mango salad spooned on top and a sprinkling of lime sugar (see recipe below).

MANGO SALAD WITH MINT AND LIME SUGAR

Serves 4-6

 15-30 MINUTES PLUS TIME TO MARINATE

Simple but oh so good. The best place to buy mangoes is in an Asian shop. Choose ones that are ripe but not too ripe or they'll turn to mush when you cut them.

2 medium to large ripe mangoes
2 limes, preferably unwaxed
3 tbsp unrefined caster sugar
Juice of 2 medium oranges
6-8 mint leaves

Hold each mango upright and cut vertically down each side as near as you can get to the stone. Peel the slices you've made then cut away the rest of the flesh from around the stone. Cut into chunks, saving the juice. Grate the rind of one of the limes and mix with 1 tbsp of the caster sugar.

Set aside. Squeeze the juice from both limes and both oranges and mix together. Sweeten with the remaining sugar. Tip the mango pieces and their juice into the mixed fruit juice and mix together well. Cut the mint leaves into fine strips, add them to the salad then cover with clingfilm and refrigerate till needed (don't make this more than 2-3 hours ahead). Divide the mango between individual glass dishes, spoon over the juice and the mint and sprinkle the lime sugar over the top. Or serve as described with the Pink Coconut Rice (see opposite).

- If you take the view that life is too short to peel a mango you can buy packs of ready-diced mango in the supermarket. More expensive obviously and it won't taste quite as good but it will save you time.

FRESH PINEAPPLE WITH RUM, LIME AND CHILLI Serves 6

 **PREPARATION AND COOKING TIME: UNDER 15 MINUTES PLUS CHILLING TIME**

This combination of ingredients might sound wildly unlikely but believe me it works! The chilli is optional but surprisingly good. You could always serve it in a separate bowl for people to add their own if you feel a bit nervy about it.

1 medium ripe pineapple
Juice of 2 fresh limes (about 4 tbsp)
3 tbsp white or golden rum
3-4 tbsp caster sugar
1 mild red chilli, de-seeded and very finely sliced and/or a few shakes of a chilli-flavoured spice grind (optional)

First prepare the pineapple. Cut the leaves off the top then cut it across in half. With the cut side downwards cut away the skin with a sharp knife, then remove the little brown bits that are left with the point of a sharp knife (fiddly but worth it for the taste). Cut each pineapple half into quarters and cut away the central core, then slice each quarter very finely and put it in a bowl. Pour over the lime juice and rum and sprinkle with sugar, and then mix together carefully with a couple of big spoons. Cover and chill till needed. To serve lay the pineapple slices on a large flat dish and sprinkle with fine slices of chilli or a some freshly ground spices from the spice grind. Serve on its own or with tofu (or vanilla) ice cream.

The following recipes are devised to please not only fellow veggies, but your meat-eating friends as well. Soup is much underrated as a dinner party starter. You rarely get offered it in restaurants nowadays, so a good one is a treat.

LUXURY CARAMELISED CAULIFLOWER SOUP

Serves 6   **15-30 MINUTES**

You simply won't believe cauliflower could taste so sumptuous – or that there's no cream in this luxurious soup, which was inspired by the brilliant Heston Blumenthal (see also p135). You only need a small bowl – it's so rich.

1 medium to large cauliflower
75g unsalted butter
1/4 tsp curry powder, plus a little extra for decoration
150ml semi-skimmed milk
600ml light vegetable stock made with 2 rounded tsp Marigold vegetable bouillon powder or an organic vegetable stock cube
Salt, black pepper and lemon juice to taste

Trim the base and the leaves off the cauliflower, break into florets then chop them finely. Cut the butter into cubes, put them in a large saucepan and place on a medium to high heat. Add the cauliflower and cook, stirring occasionally until golden brown (about 12-15 minutes). Stir in the curry powder and cook for another 2-3 minutes then add the milk, and bring to the boil, stirring. Reduce the heat, cover the pan and simmer for 5 minutes. Add 300ml of the stock, bring to the boil again then cook gently until the cauliflower is soft (about another 5 minutes). Remove the pan from the heat, leave to stand for 5 minutes then tip the contents into a liquidiser and purée until smooth. Scoop the purée out of the blender and return to the pan. Whizz up the remaining stock in the blender to pick up the last bits and add to the cauliflower purée. Stir well and re-heat gently. Season to taste with lemon juice and black pepper then add as much salt as you think the soup needs. Serve in small bowls with some cut chives over the top and a sprinkle of curry powder (see footnote).

- Chives look more interesting if you cut them in longer lengths rather than chopping them finely.
- To sprinkle curry powder take a pinch between your thumb and forefinger and rub them gently together over the soup bowl so you get little dots of powder over the soup.

WHITE VELVET SOUP

Serves 6 30 MINUTES – 1 HOUR

It was my elder daughter who named this soup which I was otherwise going to call white bean, garlic and rosemary soup. 'That doesn't sound sexy enough', she pronounced. 'It really ought to be in the aphrodisiac section'. Well I couldn't quite squeeze it in there but she has a point. Just halve the recipe if you want to make it for two.

1 level tsp vegan bouillon powder or half an organic vegetable stock cube
3 sprigs of fresh rosemary or 5 small sprigs of fresh thyme
4 tbsp olive oil
2 medium to large onions (about 225g), peeled and roughly chopped
2 large cloves of garlic, peeled and roughly chopped
2 x 400g cans of cannellini beans, drained and rinsed
1/4 tsp mushroom ketchup (optional)
Salt and freshly ground black pepper
2 tbsp finely chopped parsley or a few chopped chives
A few drops of white truffle flavoured extra virgin olive oil

Put the bouillon powder or stock cube and the rosemary in a measuring jug and pour over boiling water to the 600ml mark. Cover the jug with a saucer and leave to infuse. Heat the oil over a moderate heat in a large saucepan, add the onions and garlic and stir well. Turn the heat down, cover the pan and leave to cook on a low heat for about 10 minutes. Drain the beans in a colander or sieve and rinse well under cold running water. Tip the beans into the chopped onion and garlic and add just enough strained stock to cover, making sure the rosemary sprigs don't fall in. Bring up to the boil and cook for another 10 minutes until the beans are soft. Remove the pan from the heat and cool for 10 minutes then whizz up in batches in a blender or food processor, pouring the finished soup into a clean saucepan. Strain the remaining stock into the blender together with another 250ml of water and whizz to clean up all the remaining bits of bean purée. Pour this into the soup then bring it back to the boil and season to taste with salt, pepper and a few drops of mushroom ketchup if you have some. Dilute with a little extra water if it seems too thick. Ladle the soup into bowls, scatter over a little chopped parsley and trickle over a thin drizzle of truffle oil.

• Truffle oil may seem extravagant but think of it like perfume. The aroma – and flavour – are divine and you only need a tiny amount. Try it with a shop-bought mushroom soup too or with mashed potato!

If you want a satisfyingly savoury main course that will keep carnivorous friends happy, it's hard to beat mushrooms.

MIDNIGHT MUSHROOMS

Serves 4-6 15-30 MINUTES

I called this dish Midnight Mushroooms because of its exotic, smoky flavour, assisted by a secret ingredient no-one will guess: a pinch of lapsang souchong tea leaves.

750g portabella or large flat mushrooms
2 tbsp olive oil
A small slice (about 15g) butter (or an extra tbsp oil)
1 medium to large onion, peeled and roughly chopped
2 cloves of garlic, peeled and crushed
1 level tsp sweet Spanish pimenton or 1 tsp paprika
1/4 tsp ground lapsang souchong tea leaves (optional)
100ml medium dry montilla, sherry or tawny port
150l instant miso soup or stock made with 1 level tsp dark miso or Marmite
1-2 tbsp tomato ketchup or passata
Salt and freshly ground black pepper

Rinse the mushrooms under running water, rubbing off any loose earth or grit. Slice them thickly. Heat a large saucepan or casserole over a low heat and add the oil. Heat for another minute or two and add the butter (if using). Add the onion, stir, cover the pan and cook for 5 minutes until soft. Stir in the crushed garlic and paprika and lapsang souchong (if using) and cook for another minute. Pour in the montilla, bubble up, then add the mushrooms and mix thoroughly. Cook for another 3-4 minutes till the liquid has evaporated (don't panic if it looks dry) then add the stock. Cover the pan and cook over a low heat for about 10 minutes until the mushrooms have created their own sauce, then remove the lid and let the sauce simmer for about 5 minutes. Check seasoning, adding salt, pepper and tomato ketchup or passata to taste. Serve with Yummy Polenta (see below) or a Half-Baked Potato (see p86) and a spinach, rocket and watercress salad.

YUMMY POLENTA

Serves 4-6 15-30 MINUTES

Polenta is made from corn. It doesn't have much flavour itself so you need to add immoderate amounts of butter and Parmesan to it to make a delectable, sloppy, cheesy goo.

1 litre of vegetable stock made with 1 tbsp vegetable bouillon powder or a vegetable stock cube
175g good quality Italian polenta
75g butter at room temperature
40g freshly grated Parmesan
Salt and freshly ground black pepper

Bring I litre of stock to the boil in a big (preferably non-stick) saucepan then reduce to a simmer. Tip the polenta into a jug then gradually add it to the simmering stock, whisking all the time. Continue stirring until it begins to thicken then turn the heat right down and cook for about 15-20 minutes until really thick, stirring it every couple of minutes. Add the butter, bit by bit, then add the cheese. Season to taste with salt and pepper.

• This is one of those dishes where ingredients are everything. Try and buy both your polenta and your Parmesan from an Italian deli.

OPEN LASAGNA WITH PORCINI AND CHESTNUT MUSHROOMS

Serves 6 as a starter
30 MINUTES – 1 HOUR

This not only has the virtue of being wildly impressive – it's also much, much easier than a conventional lasagne.

25g pack dried porcini
250g chestnut mushrooms
1 tbsp olive oil
A small lump of butter (about 10g)
Half a 300g tub ready-made fresh cheese sauce
  (e.g. four cheese sauce)
2 tbsp low-fat crème fraîche
Freshly ground black pepper
A good squeeze of lemon juice
20g pack flat leaf parsley, finely chopped
6 sheets of fresh lasagne (from the chill cabinet)
1 tbsp freshly grated Parmesan

Soak the porcini for 30 minutes in enough warm water to cover. Carefully strain off the liquid into a bowl and set to one side. Roughly chop the porcini. Wipe and slice the chestnut mushrooms quite thickly (about 5 slices from a large mushroom, 4 from smaller ones). Heat the oil in a large frying pan, add the butter and when it starts foaming chuck in the fresh mushrooms and stir them around for 2 or 3 minutes until they start to colour and soften. Add the soaked dried mushrooms, turn up the heat and cook for another 2 minutes or until the liquid has evaporated. Stir in the cheese sauce and crème fraîche. Add a little of the water you used to soak the mushrooms to the sauce – about 2 tbsp. Season to taste with black pepper and a good squeeze of lemon and stir in half the chopped parsley. Keep warm while you cook the lasagne briefly in a large pan of salted boiling water with a few drops of oil in it (about 1 1/2 minutes from when the water comes back to the boil). Drain. Working quickly so the lasagne sheets don't get cold lay each sheet out on a warm plate. Spoon a sixth of the mushroom mixture on one half and fold the other half casually over the top. (You don't want the edges neatly lined up.) Sprinkle with a little Parmesan and a bit of the remaining parsley. Repeat with the other sheets of pasta and serve.

It's easy of course to buy a perfectly acceptable pud in a supermarket or upmarket deli but if you want to knock the socks off your guests make one of these.

STRAWBERRY PAVLOVA
Serves 4-6
OVER 1 HOUR

This is one of those retro puddings whose appeal never seems to fade. I originally got the recipe from a cookery writer called Nicola Cox and I haven't found a better one. It just looks and tastes fantastic.

3 large egg whites (see p65)
175g caster sugar plus 2-3 extra tsp for
   sweetening the cream
1/2-1 tsp vanilla extract or essence plus a few
   extra drops for the cream
3/4 tsp white malt or wine vinegar
1 tsp cornflour
500g ripe strawberries
284 ml carton of double cream

You will need some non-stick baking parchment – and a hand-held electric beater if you don't want to give yourself repetitive strain injury whipping the egg whites. Pre-heat the oven to 150C/300F/Gas 2. Roll out the baking parchment. Take a large plate, turn it upside down on the paper and draw round it with a pencil or pen then cut round the circle you've made. Place it on a baking sheet. Whisk the egg whites in a deep bowl until just holding their shape. Gradually whisk in one third of the sugar then keep whisking until the mixture is very stiff and shiny. Fold in* the remaining sugar, then finally fold in the vanilla essence, vinegar and cornflour (sieved over the top of the mixture to avoid lumps). Spoon the meringue onto the circle of paper hollowing out the centre slightly so the edges are higher than the middle. Bake for about 1 hour until the top is pale golden brown. When cool enough to handle (about 10 minutes) carefully peel off the baking parchment then leave to get completely cold. De-stalk and slice the strawberries. Whip the cream (it should hold its shape but not be stiff). Add 1/2 tsp vanilla extract and 2 tsp caster sugar and fold carefully into the cream. Pile half the cream onto the Pavlova, top with half the strawberries then spoon over the remaining cream and arrange the rest of the strawberries artistically over the top.

- To 'fold' one ingredient into another, use a big serving spoon and take it down through the mixture in vertical movements, scooping the ingredients at the bottom up to the top.

Cheat's mini-pavs
If you want to make an easy version of this buy six meringue nests (Marks and Sparks do very good ones), fill them with sweetened whipped cream or vanilla ice cream and top with sliced strawberries.

SIMPLE, BRILLIANT CHOCOLATE 'MOUSSE' Serves 6-8

 UNDER 15 MINUTES

You're simply not going to believe how easy this recipe is. Or how much fun it is to make. I found it in Heston Blumenthal's Family Food, *a great book from a great young chef who's just won three Michelin stars. He in turn got it from a French chemist called Hervé This. Heston calls it Hervé's Chocolate Chantilly but to me it just tastes like the best imaginable chocolate mousse.*

230ml water
270g best quality bitter chocolate*

You will need a hand-held electric whisk or chef's balloon whisk for this. Measure the water carefully – quantitites are critical in this recipe. (Measure to the 250ml mark then take out 1 tbsp and 1 tsp of water). Break up the chocolate into squares, put it in a saucepan with the water and put it over a low heat, stirring occasionally until it has melted. Meanwhile get two bowls, one slightly smaller than the other. Put some cold water and ice cubes in the larger one then place the smaller one inside it. Have your whisk ready. When the chocolate has melted pour it into the smaller bowl and start to beat it on the highest setting of your whisk or energetically by hand. After a few minutes (about 2-3) it will thicken and begin to go like whipped cream. Your beaters should leave a

slight trail in the chocolate but it shouldn't be stiff. Take the small bowl out of the big bowl and spoon the 'mousse' into small coffee cups or glasses. (That might sound mean but it is unbelievably rich!) If you do overbeat it simply tip the chocolate back into the saucepan, melt it and start again.

• Look for dark chocolate that contains about 70% cocoa solids for this. Lindt Excellence is a good brand or use a Belgian dark chocolate.

You don't need me to tell you there's something wonderfully sensuous about eating with your hands. (Or can be – I exclude a bag of chips or a petrol station sandwich.) So this menu is largely planned around dishes you can dip, dunk or simply put your fingers into and lick. It also has the virtue of requiring minimal preparation leaving you free to do more interesting things...

ASPARAGUS WITH LEMON AND BUTTER DIP Serves 2
UNDER 15 MINUTES

Asparagus is regarded as an aphrodisiac for obvious reasons but is also one of the best veggie treats you can eat with your fingers.

250g asparagus
50g butter
2 tbsp lemon juice

Plunge the asparagus into a sink or bowl of cold water and give it a good shake to clean. With a sharp knife cut off the tough end of the stalk (about $1/3$ of the way up the spear). Lay the spears in the top of a steamer and steam for 4 minutes or until you can easily insert a sharp knife into the stalks. Alternatively lay them in a microwaveable dish with a couple of tablespoons of water, cover with a damp piece of kitchen towel (just soak it under a running tap and lay it carefully over the dish) and microwave on high for about $3^1/2$ minutes.

Meanwhile melt the butter gently in a saucepan and stir in the lemon juice. Pour into a bowl and dunk the asparagus spears as you eat them.

MOLTEN CAMEMBERT
Serves 2 **15-30 MINUTES**

I've seen variations on this all over the place but you really don't need to add anything to it. The original comes from the brilliant Nigel Slater's Real Food.

1 camembert in a wooden box
1 clove of garlic, peeled and halved (optional)
Freshly ground black pepper

Heat the oven to 200C/400F/Gas 6. Remove any plastic wrapping from the cheese and replace it in the box. Rub the cut sides of the garlic over the surface of the cheese. Stab a few holes in the top of the cheese and replace the lid. Bake for about 25 minutes until molten. Serve with crusty bread, breadsticks and, if you're feeling particularly sinful, tiny, boiled baby new potatoes to dunk in it.

GOOEY CHEESE FONDUE
POTATOES Serves 2
15-30 MINUTES

*This was originally conceived as a solo pleasure
but it also makes great post-sex eating for two.
With a simple green salad if you have the energy
to make one.*

300g tiny, boiled new potatoes
150g mature Cheddar cheese
2 level tsp plain flour
5-6 tbsp milk
A few chives
Salt and freshly ground black pepper

Bring a pan of water to the boil (use a kettle to
boil the water – it's quicker). Add salt and the
potatoes and cook for about 12-15 minutes until
you can easily stick the point of a knife into them.
Drain. Meanwhile grate the cheese and put it in
another saucepan. Mix in the flour and the milk
and heat very gently until it turns into a smooth
sauce (about 2-3 minutes). Season with salt and
pepper. Divide the potatoes between two plates
and pour over the cheese sauce. Snip the chives
over the top. You can use fingers to eat them with
but a fork is probably easier.

Other good dishes to seduce with
- Spring Vegetable Risotto p112.
- White Velvet Soup p131.
- Open Lasagna with Porcini and Chestnut
  Mushrooms p133.

Personally, I'd pass on a main course and go straight on to a sweet. Or two.

CHOCOLATE-DIPPED STRAWBERRIES Serves 2
UNDER 15 MINUTES (LESS WHEN STRAWBERRIES ARE IN SEASON)

This is such a simple recipe you'll want to make it all the time once strawberries are in season. Around Valentine's Day – the time you're most likely to think about it – take care buying your strawberries. You want ones that are bright red all over. The ones that are white round the stalk are underripe and will taste a bit sharp.

A small carton of ripe, firm strawberries (about 225g)
100g dark luxury Belgian chocolate (see footnote)

Break the chocolate into a small bowl and perch it over a saucepan with a little boiling water in the base. Make sure the bottom of the bowl doesn't touch the water. Stir the chocolate until it melts. Lay a piece of greaseproof paper or lightly greased foil on a baking tray or large plate that will fit in the fridge. Pick up a strawberry by the stalk and dunk it in the chocolate about half to two thirds up the fruit so you leave some red showing. Lay it on the paper or foil. When you've finished the strawberries, chill them for 20-30 minutes in the fridge. Lick the bowl.

• Supermarkets sell Belgian chocolate in the baking section. It's a lot cheaper than good quality eating chocolate and sweeter than the ones that have higher proportions of cocoa solids. You could also make it with white chocolate.

LEMON MASCARPONE DIP
Serves 2 **UNDER 15 MINUTES**

The idea struck me recently that if you have savoury dips there's no reason why you shouldn't have sweet ones. Mascarpone makes the perfect base. Combine it with some puréed fruit or a fruit-based curd and within seconds you have something that tastes like liquid cheesecake.

125g Mascarpone
2 heaped tbsp (about 75g) good quality lemon curd, home-made if possible (by someone else, not you! Visit a WI market – see p11)
1-2 tbsp freshly squeezed lemon juice
A few ripe strawberries
Sponge finger (Savoiardi) biscuits or thin, crisp little ginger biscuits

Tip the Mascarpone into a bowl and mash with a fork. Gradually work in the lemon curd and beat until smooth. Add 1 tbsp of lemon juice and taste. Add more lemon if you want it sharper and a little sugar if you find it too tart. Add 2 tbsp of water to thin it to a dipping consistency then chill it until you're ready to eat. Serve with strawberries and sponge fingers or crisp ginger biscuits.

SWEET WINE AND DIPPING BISCUITS

More an idea than a recipe. This is how many Italians would finish a meal on a special occasion. The classic wine to use would be Vin Santo but that tends to be very expensive. The Greeks make a much cheaper one called Visanto (available at Oddbins) which is just as delicious. Or use an inexpensive southern French or Greek sweet muscat wine. As I've mentioned already (p13) not all wines are suitable for vegetarians so you'll need to check. Then just chill the wine and serve in small pretty glasses with a plate of Italian cantucci (almond flavoured biscuits) to dunk in it.

AFFOGATO

Serves 2 **UNDER 15 MINUTES**

A sophisticated dessert for lovers of strong, espresso coffee though don't be scared off. It tastes milder once the espresso mingles with the ice cream. Don't on any account try to make it with instant coffee – buy a takeaway triple espresso from a café with an espresso machine.

4 scoops of home-made or top quality bought
 vanilla ice cream e.g. Hill Station
75ml strong espresso coffee
2 tbsp Kahlua or other coffee liqueur

Put two scoops of ice cream in two cups or glasses. Warm the Kahlua with the coffee until hot but not boiling and pour over the ice cream.

- For other sweet treats take a look at the dessert pages of the Eat Italian, Go Greek and Try Thai sections (obviously you'll have to adjust quantitites). For the morning after, see also Winter and Summer Breakfast ideas on pp70-73, and pancakes over the page....

Anyone who has never made a pancake will think they're extremely difficult (and therefore impressive). You, once you've made them, will know they're not. Once you've mastered the basic technique you can run them up any time you want an instant pudding or something impressive for brunch.

AMERICAN BREAKFAST PANCAKES WITH FRESH BERRIES AND FROMAGE FRAIS Makes about 12 pancakes

UNDER 15 MINUTES

A good place to start with pancakes.
Easy to make. Easy to flip. Delicious.

400g strawberries or 250g fresh raspberries or
  blueberries
A large tub of low-fat fromage frais or Greek
  yoghurt
For the pancakes
40g of butter
125g plain flour
1/4 level tsp salt
2 level tsp caster sugar
1 1/2 level tsp baking powder
1 large fresh free-range egg
150ml whole (i.e. not skimmed or semi-skimmed)
  milk

First check if the fruit needs sweetening (strawberries probably will out of season. Just take off the stalks, slice them thickly and sprinkle with a tablespoon of sugar). To make the pancakes: melt the butter in a saucepan over a low heat and set aside to cool. Sieve the flour, salt and baking powder into a bowl, mix in the sugar then form a hollow in the centre with the back of a wooden spoon. Lightly beat the egg, mix with the milk and a tablespoon of the melted butter and gradually pour into the flour, working it into the liquid with your spoon and beating it until it forms a thick batter. Don't worry if it looks a bit lumpy. Heat a non-stick frying pan over a moderate heat, pour in a little of the remaining melted butter and spread it over the pan with a piece of kitchen towel. Place four tablespoons of the pancake mixture into the pan, leaving a space between them. Let them cook for about a minute until bubbles begin to appear on the surface, then flip them over with a spatula and cook them for 45 seconds on the other side. Stack them on a plate covered with a clean tea-towel and repeat the process until all the mixture is used up, greasing the pan with melted butter before you cook each batch. Arrange 3 pancakes on each plate, spoon some fruit alongside and top with a dollop of fromage frais or yoghurt. You could also offer some runny honey to drizzle over the top for the sweet-toothed.

CLASSIC PANCAKE DAY PANCAKES

Makes about 6-8 26cm (10 inch) pancakes

30 MINUTES

These are bigger pancakes, the kind you flip (or drop).

110g plain flour, preferably organic
1/4 tsp salt
2 large fresh free-range eggs
275ml semi-skimmed milk
25g cooled melted butter plus another 25g butter
    for greasing the pan

For serving
2 juicy lemons cut into quarters
Granulated sugar

Sieve the flour and salt into a large bowl. Make a hollow in the centre. Beat the eggs lightly with the milk then add 25g of cooled butter. Gradually pour the mixture into the flour, stirring as you go and beat it until you have a smooth thin batter. Set it aside for 30 minutes then beat again. (If you have a food processor just place the flour, salt, eggs and half the milk in a food processor, whiz, then slowly add the remaining milk.) Heat the pan for about 2 minutes until quite hot then grease it with some scrunched-up kitchen towel dipped in the remaining butter. Scoop out a small cup or 1/3 of a mug of batter and tip it into the pan, tilting it and swirling it round quickly so the whole base of the pan is covered with batter. Cook for about 30 seconds till the edges begin to brown then flip over with a spatula and cook the other side (see footnote). Serve up straight away as you make them, squeezing on lemon and sprinkling with about a teaspoon of granulated sugar, then rolling them up or folding them into four.

- If you want to be really flashy and toss them, ease a spatula round the sides of the pancake to make sure it's not stuck to the bottom. Give the pan a good shake then holding the handle with both hands jerk it upwards, so that the pancake flips over and lands safely (you pray) in the pan. Be prepared to move the pan to catch it in mid-flight and don't try to toss it too high!
- It really helps to have a proper pan for making pancakes – a low-sided pancake pan, about 24-26cm wide. The best time to buy one is in the run up to pancake day when shops tend to have them on special offer. Failing that a large clean non-stick frying pan will do, though I realise that's a tall order....
- You can also serve these pancakes with a savoury filling such as cooked spinach, Ricotta and Parmesan cheese, sliced mushrooms fried in butter and garlic with a spoonful of cream or Stir-Fried Peppers (see p36). They also taste good if you replace half the flour with wholewheat flour or, even better, buckwheat flour (available from health food shops).

I have to confess I'm not a great fan of nut roasts, the usual Christmas fare for veggies, but you'll find plenty of recipes online if you want to make one from scratch. Or ready-made ones in the supermarket. But have a go at this festive couscous instead. It really does look beautiful.

FESTIVE FIG AND CHESTNUT COUSCOUS Serves 4

 30 MINUTES

I made this last year for the veggies at our Christmas lunch but all the meat-eaters kept loading their plates up with it too so there wasn't quite enough. If you suspect the same thing will happen make double the quantity!

5 medium or 3 large carrots (about 350g), peeled
3 sticks of celery
4 tbsp sunflower or light olive oil
2 medium onions, peeled and roughly chopped
300g tinned, vacuum packed or frozen chestnuts
175g ready-to-eat figs
3 tbsp dairy-free spread
1½ tsp of ground mixed spice
Salt
150g instant couscous
1 pomegranate (optional)
3 tbsp finely chopped fresh parsley

Cut the carrots across the middle and finely slice the bottom halves. Cut the top halves into two lengthways and cut them into thin slices too. Wash and trim the tops and bottoms off the celery and cut into thin slices. Heat a casserole or large frying pan, add the oil and cook the chopped onion, carrot and celery for about 7-8 minutes until beginning to soften and brown. Add half a glass (about 100 ml) of water, and cook for about another 10 minutes until the vegetables are tender and the water has evaporated. (Add a little more water if they dry out.) Meanwhile finely chop the chestnuts and the figs. Turn up the heat in the pan and add the dairy-free spread. Let it melt then add the chestnuts and figs, stir and fry for a couple of minutes. Sprinkle over the spice, season with salt and stir again. Turn the heat right down, add the couscous and 150ml of boiling water, stir then leave for 5 minutes for the couscous to absorb the water. Meanwhile cut the pomegranate in half and scoop out the seeds, leaving the pith behind. Fork the couscous through, check the seasoning, adding more salt if necessary and stir in the chopped parsley. Serve on a big plate with the pomegranate seeds scattered over the top.

MULLED CHRISTMAS CRUMBLE

Serves 4 **30 MINUTES – 1 HOUR**

This combines two of my favourite things – mulled wine (or rather port) and crumble. Look for a Vintage Character or Special Reserve port which is smoother and more drinkable than a basic ruby port. Own label is fine – you should be able to find plenty on special offer in the run-up to Christmas.

1 small jar of cranberry sauce or about 3 large dollops home-made cranberry sauce if you feel inspired to make some
3 tbsp Vintage Character or Special Reserve port
1½ tsp mixed spice
A fine slice of orange peel
1 500g pack Black Forest Fruits or other frozen red berries
Extra sugar to taste

For the crumble topping
175g plain flour
1 tsp cinnamon or mixed spice
100g chilled butter from the fridge
60g (about 4 tbsp) unrefined caster sugar

Tip the cranberry sauce in a saucepan, add the port and heat gently until it has melted. Stir in the spice, add the orange peel then tip in the frozen fruit, bring to the boil, stir then set aside to infuse. Measure the flour and cinnamon, or mixed spice (if using) into a large bowl. Cut the butter into small cubes and tip it into the flour. Keep cutting until you can't get the pieces of butter any smaller then rub the butter and flour together with the tips of your fingers, lifting it up and letting it fall back again into the bowl until the mixture is the consistency of coarse breadcrumbs. Stir in the sugar and carry on rubbing for another minute. (You can do this in seconds in a food processor.) Heat the oven to 200C/400F/Gas 6. Remove the orange rind from the fruit and check them for sweetness, adding more sugar if you think they need it. Tip them into a lightly buttered or oiled baking dish. Spread the crumble mixture evenly over the fruit making sure you cover the whole surface, then bake for about 30-35 minutes till the crumble is brown and the fruit juices bubbling round the sides of the dish. Serve with vanilla ice cream or cream.

- Greasing a baking dish before cooking makes washing up a lot easier! Just take a piece of kitchen towel, dip it in soft butter, dairy-free spread or a flavourless oil and rub it round the inside of the dish.
- If you wanted to bulk up the filling you could add a peeled, finely sliced Bramley apple to the fruit.
- See also Cheat's Christmas pudding from *Beyond Baked Beans*. (Veggie Christmas pudding, of course....)

BAKING THERAPY

Remember when you were little, messing around in the kitchen? The first thing you probably made were some biscuits or fairy cakes. Why? Because the ingredients were cheap and to hand in the cupboard, it was easy and above all oh-so-rewarding when the smell of baking filled the kitchen and you could eat your mis-shapen masterpieces warm and crumbly straight from the oven. No shop-bought cake or biscuit ever tastes as good as that.

So why not bake again now? You can afford it and it will make you feel good. You will instantly double your number of friends. Good news all round.

You don't have to be a genius to do it. You just need a bit of basic kit – cake tins, a couple of baking trays, baking parchment (so things don't stick), scales and measuring spoons. Measurements matter in baking. You can pick them all up cheaply in supermarkets or charity shops – just add to your collection bit by bit.

Go on, treat yourself....

Unlike most of the other recipes in this book quantities matter with baking, so if I give a precise measurement or recommend a particular size of tin it's to make sure it works. Oven temperatures vary, so you may need a slightly longer or shorter cooking time.

CRUNCHY NUT FLAPJACKS

Makes 16 bars 🍁 **30 MINUTES – 1 HOUR (PLUS COOLING TIME)**

You should let these harden, but you might not be able to resist devouring them whilst soft and crumbly.

125g dairy-free margarine or spread (or butter if you're not vegan)
75g unsweetened crunchy peanut butter (e.g. Whole Earth)
175g demerara sugar
2 tbsp golden syrup
75g (3 oz) shelled, unsalted roasted peanuts
225g porridge oats, preferably organic

You will need a small rectangular baking tin (about 27cm x 17cm), lightly greased with dairy-free spread. Preheat the oven to 160C /325F/Gas 3. Place the spread, peanut butter, sugar and syrup in a heavy-bottomed saucepan and warm over a low heat until completely melted, stirring occasionally. Add the chopped peanuts and porridge oats and mix thoroughly. Spread the mixture into the tin making sure there's plenty around the sides which cook more quickly. Bake for about 35 minutes until golden brown. Remove from the oven and leave to cool for 15 minutes. Using a sharp knife mark out the bars making one cut down the length of the tin then 8 cuts across to give you 16 bars. Leave the flapjacks in the tin until they have hardened (a good 2 hours) then prise them out carefully and store in an airtight tin.

WARNING
NEVER SERVE PEANUTS OR OTHER NUTS TO ANYONE WITHOUT CHECKING WHETHER THEY'RE ALLERGIC TO THEM.

APRICOT MUESLI BARS

Makes 16 bars 🍁 **30 MINUTES – 1 HOUR (PLUS COOLING TIME)**

A delicious fruity spin on a flapjack.

175g dairy-free margarine or spread
150g dark muscovado or demerara sugar
2 tbsp golden syrup
100g dried apricots, preferably organic, cut into small pieces (easier to do with scissors!)
125g unsweetened Swiss-style muesli, preferably organic
125g porridge oats, preferably organic

You will need a small rectangular baking tin (about 27cm x 17cm), lightly greased with the dairy-free spread. Preheat the oven to 160C/325F/Gas 3. Place the spread, sugar and malt extract or syrup in a heavy-bottomed saucepan and warm over a low heat until completely melted, stirring occasionally. Add the dried apricots, muesli and rolled oats and mix thoroughly. Spread the mixture into the tin making sure there's plenty around the sides which cook more quickly. Bake for about 35 minutes until golden brown. Remove from the oven and leave to cool for 15 minutes. Using a sharp knife, mark out the bars making one cut down the length of the tin then 8 cuts across to give you 16 bars. Leave the mixture in the tin until it has hardened completely (a good 2 hours) then carefully prise out the bars and store in an airtight tin.

WARNING
NEVER SERVE PEANUTS OR OTHER NUTS TO ANYONE WITHOUT CHECKING WHETHER THEY'RE ALLERGIC TO THEM.

WARM CHOCOLATE CHIP COOKIES
Makes about 30-35 cookies
15-30 MINUTES

You can, of course, buy cookies, but the big advantage of baking them yourself is that you can eat them within minutes of taking them from the oven while the chocolate is still warm and gooey. They also make a great dessert with vanilla ice cream.

125g dark luxury Belgian chocolate
125g soft or spreadable butter (like Anchor or Lurpak)
75g soft light brown sugar
50g granulated sugar
1 large egg
$1/2$ tsp vanilla flavouring (optional)
165g plain flour
$1/2$ tsp bicarbonate of soda
$1/4$ tsp salt

You'll need at least one, preferably two baking trays. Preheat the oven to 180C/350F/Gas 4. Break the chocolate into chunks then cut it into smaller chips with a knife. Beat the butter and sugars together in a large bowl until light and fluffy. Lightly beat the egg in another bowl or mug, add the vanilla (if using) then add the egg to the butter mixture bit by bit, beating all the time. Mix in the flour, salt and bicarbonate of soda then add the chopped chocolate. Drop 8-9 teaspoons of the mixture on a baking tray leaving plenty of space in between each spoonful. Bake for 11-12 minutes until browned. Remove the tray from the oven, leave for a couple of minutes then prise off the cookies with a knife and transfer them to a wire rack (you could use an oven shelf or the rack on a grill pan). Repeat with the next batch of cookies.

- If you bake two trays at the same time the lower tray may cook more slowly than the top one, especially in a gas oven, so will need extra time.
- Try replacing the dark chocolate with white chocolate. Add 1 tbsp of sifted cocoa powder to the cookie dough when you add the flour.

DEVONSHIRE SCONES WITH CLOTTED CREAM AND JAM

Serves 4 **UNDER 30 MINUTES**

Scones are unbelievably easy once you get the hang of them. The trick is not to overwork the dough once you add the liquid.

225g plain flour plus 3 level tsp baking powder
  or 225g self raising flour plus 1 1/2 level tsp
  baking powder
A pinch of salt
60g cool, firm butter (not straight from the fridge
  but cooler than room temperature)
40g unrefined or ordinary caster sugar
1 medium to large egg
150ml milk
A small carton of clotted cream or extra thick
  double cream
Strawberry, raspberry or cherry jam

You will need a baking sheet and a scone cutter. Preheat the oven to 220C/425F/Gas 7. Put the flour, baking powder and salt into a large bowl. Cut the butter in small slices into the flour then carry on cutting it with a knife until you have very small pieces. Now get your hands into the flour and rub the butter lightly into the flour with your fingers (see footnote) until it becomes coarse and grainy. (This should take about 2-4 minutes depending how skilled you are.) Stir in the sugar. Beat the egg in a measuring jug, add milk up to the 150ml mark and beat again. Make a hollow in the flour mixture and pour in most of the egg, leaving just over a tablespoon. Using a knife, mix it in lightly and quickly drawing the mixture together, then gently press the dough together with your right (or left hand). It should be soft but not sticky – add the extra liquid if it seems too dry. Transfer the dough to a floured board or work surface and shape into a flat cake about 2.5cm deep. Stamp out rounds with a small cutter (about 2.5 cm wide) and lay them on a lightly greased baking tray. You will have to reshape the offcuts to make the last 2 or 3 scones. Brush or lightly rub the tops of the scones with the remaining egg and milk or, if you've used that, with a little extra milk and bake for about 10-12 minutes until well risen and browned. Remove from the oven, cool for 5-10 minutes then eat while still warm. Split the scones, spread the cut side with cream and top with jam.

- Rub the butter and flour between your thumbs and the tips of your first and second fingers, raising them from the bowl as you go so that the mixture gets aerated as it falls back into the bowl.
- You can add other ingredients like sultanas or chopped apple to your scones, or grated cheese for savoury scones. About 75g is enough.
- If you haven't got a scone cutter just shape the dough into a round and mark it into 8 segments with a knife. Increase the cooking time by 4-5 minutes.

BANANA AND HONEY MUFFINS

Makes 6 big muffins, or 10-12 smaller ones
PREPARATION AND COOKING TIME:
15-30 MINUTES

Muffins are one of the easiest and most delicious things to bake. You just need the kit (a muffin tin, a sieve and some paper cases if you can afford them) and the technique – light folding rather than energetic stirring or beating. If you want them to look like the ones they sell in the shops buy a deep muffin tin rather than a shallow one.

150g plain flour
1½ level tsp baking powder
½ level tsp ground cinnamon
¼ level tsp salt
50g butter
2 tbsp runny honey (about 55g)
1 heaped tbsp natural unsweetened yoghurt
About 60ml milk
½ tsp vanilla flavouring
1 large egg, lightly beaten
1 medium ripe banana (yellow rather than green
 or speckled with black)
Unrefined caster sugar for topping

You'll need a muffin tin, preferably one with deep holes. Pre-heat the oven to 190C/375F/Gas 5. Line the tin with paper cups if you have some otherwise lightly grease the pan. Sieve the flour into a bowl with the baking powder, cinnamon and salt and hollow out a dip in the centre. Gently heat the butter in a pan with the honey. Set aside and cool slightly. Put the yoghurt in a measuring jug and mix in enough milk to bring it just over the 100ml mark. Stir in the vanilla extract. Pour the honey mixture, beaten egg and yoghurt and milk into the flour, mix in lightly and swiftly with a large metal spoon to get a rough batter. (This should only take a few seconds.) Peel the banana, slice it thinly into the batter and stir lightly so that all the slices are coated. Spoon the batter into the muffin tin and sprinkle with a little caster sugar. Bake for 25-30 minutes (15-20 minutes if your muffins are smaller) or until fully risen and well browned. Leave in the tin or paper cups for 5 minutes then put on a cooling rack.

A PROPER OLD-FASHIONED CHOCOLATE CAKE LIKE YOUR GRAN USED TO MAKE...

Serves 6-8 **UNDER 1 HOUR**

...and may very well still do so. This is called the all-in-one method for the logical reason that you put all the ingredients in a bowl at the same time rather than adding them step by step as with most cakes. The chocolatey flavour also comes from cocoa rather than expensive dark chocolate. Which makes it both easy and economical.

2 rounded tbsp cocoa powder (15g)
175g self-raising flour
1½ level tsp baking powder
175g unrefined caster sugar
175g spreadable butter at room temperatue
3 medium-sized fresh free-range eggs
For the chocolate fudge icing
75g icing sugar
25g cocoa powder
40g butter
50g unrefined caster sugar

You will need 2 x 18cm round cake tins, lightly oiled and lined with a circle of baking paper. Preheat the oven to 160C/350F/Gas 4. Measure the cocoa powder into a cup and pour over 3 tbsp of boiling water. Stir until smooth and set aside. Sift the flour and the baking powder into a large bowl, add the sugar and the butter. Break the eggs into a large cup or small bowl, mix lightly with a fork and pour that into the big bowl as well. With a wooden spoon or hand-held electric beaters mix the ingredients together beating them until smooth. (They will look alarmingly lumpy to begin with but come together quite easily in about a minute.) Divide the mixture between the two cake tins and smooth it across the surface with a rubber spatula or a flat-bladed knife, leave a slight dip in the middle so it rises evenly. Lick the bowl (the best bit). Put the tins in the oven and bake for 25 minutes checking them half way through. (One tin may take slightly longer than the other if you have an elderly or temperamental oven. You can tell if the cake is done as it will have shrunk away slightly from the sides of the tin and spring back if you press gently on the surface.) Take the tins out of the oven, leave them to cool for 5 minutes then run a knife round the inside of each tin to ensure the cake hasn't stuck, turn the tin upside down and tip each cake onto a cooling rack. Carefully peel off the paper on the bottom and leave to cool for about 20-25 minutes. Meanwhile, make the icing: sift the icing sugar and the cocoa powder into a bowl. Put the butter, sugar and 2 tbsp of water in a saucepan and heat over a low heat stirring occasionally until the sugar has dissolved. Bring the sugar and butter mix to the boil and pour over the icing sugar and cocoa powder and beat well until smooth. Leave to cool, beating occasionally until it begins to thicken and lighten in colour. Put one half of the cake on a plate, bottom side upwards, spread with half the icing then place the other half of the cake on top, bottom side downwards. Spread and swirl the remaining icing over the cake and leave for as long as you can bear it to harden.

DAVID'S GORGEOUS GINGER CAKE
Serves 6-8 **OVER 1 HOUR**

A brilliant first-time baker's recipe from my friend David Herbert's The Perfect Cookbook.

60g butter, cubed
125g golden syrup
100g plain flour
25g self-raising flour
1 tsp bicarbonate of soda
1 heaped tsp ground ginger
1/2 tsp mixed spice
100g caster sugar
Pinch of salt
125ml milk
1 egg, beaten
For the syrup
125g sugar
A small chunk of ginger, peeled and grated
  (makes about 1tbsp)

Thoroughly grease a 23 x 12cm loaf tin and line the base with baking paper. Preheat the oven to 170C/365F/Gas mark 3. Put the butter and golden syrup in a small saucepan. Melt, stirring

occasionally, over a low heat, then remove from the heat. Sift both flours, the soda and the spices into a mixing bowl. Stir in the sugar and salt, then add the milk and egg, and mix until smooth. Gradually add the melted-butter mixture, stirring until well incorporated. Pour the batter into the loaf tin and bake for 50-55 minutes, or until risen and firm to the touch. A skewer inserted into the middle of the cake should come out clean. Allow the cake to cool in the tin for 5 minutes before turning out on to a wire rack to cool. Make a syrup by placing the sugar, 125ml water and the finely grated ginger into a small saucepan. Bring it to the boil and simmer for 5 minutes. Spoon a little syrup over the hot cake and leave to cool.

• If you haven't time to make the syrup, just sprinkle the cake with a little sifted icing sugar.

IRISH SODA BREAD

Serves 4-6
30 MINUTES – 1 HOUR

If you've never made bread in your life you could make Irish soda bread. It requires no kneading or rising time – you can make it from start to finish inside an hour. Everyone's version differs slightly. This is based on the recipe that baker Dan Lepard gives in Baking with Passion.

284 ml carton buttermilk or very low fat bio
  yoghurt
1 level tbsp black treacle
225g self-raising flour
225g plain wholemeal flour (not bread flour)
  plus extra for dusting
1 tbsp wheatgerm
$1/2$ level tsp cream of tartar
1 level tsp bicarbonate of soda
1 rounded tsp fine sea salt

Preheat the oven to 190C/375F/Gas 5. Warm the buttermilk very gently in a pan with the treacle until the treacle melts, stir well then take it off the heat. Combine the dry ingredients in a large mixing bowl. Pour over the milk and treacle mixture and mix with a wooden spoon then pull the mixture together with your hands, trickling in a little water as needed. The dough should be soft but not sticky. Shape the dough into a ball about 18cm wide and place on a floured baking tray. Cut a deep cross in the centre of the loaf, dust with a little more flour and bake for about 35-40 minutes until the bread is well browned and the bottom of the loaf sounds hollow when you tap it. Transfer onto a wire rack, cover with a clean tea-towel to stop the crust getting too hard, and cool for about 20-30 minutes. Serve while still warm.

Buying a breadmaker

If you want a really fun toy to play with in the kitchen it's hard to beat a breadmaker. Nowadays you can buy them for between £30-£40 so it may be something you want to put on your wish list 1if you move into a student house. The best bit about it is that you can pre-set it to bake so that you have a loaf ready when you come down in the morning. Always assuming you get up....

HOT CHILLI CORNBREAD

Serves 6 **30 MINUTES – 1 HOUR**

Hot in two senses – it includes chilli and it's served warm and crumbly, straight from the oven. Cornbreads are very popular in the southern states of America where they often make them in a cast iron frying pan – as you can too if you've got one that will go in the oven.

25g butter
2 tbsp olive oil plus a little extra for greasing the cake tin
1/2 a pack of spring onions, peeled and finely chopped
2 mild red chillies or 1 red and one green chilli, de-seeded and finely chopped
150g fine cornmeal plus a little extra for coating the tin
110g plain flour
2 1/2 tsp baking powder
3/4 tsp sea salt
1/2 tsp chilli powder
2 heaped tbsp plain low-fat yoghurt
About 100ml semi-skimmed milk
2 medium eggs or 1 large egg
2 tbsp freshly grated Parmesan (optional)

You'll need a small round cake tin (about 18 cm wide), lightly greased and lined with a circle of non-stick baking parchment. Pre-heat the oven to 200C/400F/Gas 6. Heat a small saucepan, add the butter and oil and fry the chopped spring onions and chillies gently for about 4 minutes until beginning to soften. Set aside while you prepare the other ingredients. Measure out the cornmeal into a bowl then sieve in the flour, baking powder, sea salt and chilli powder. Mix together leaving a slight hollow in the centre. Put the yoghurt in a measuring jug, and pour in milk up to the 250ml mark. Mix together then break in the eggs and mix them in too. Pour the liquid into the dry ingredients along with the butter, onions and chilli (and Parmesan, if using) and beat together lightly with a wooden spoon. Sprinkle a little cornmeal over the base and sides of the tin then pour in the bread mix and spread level with a spatula. Bake in the pre-heated oven for about 20-25 minutes until well risen and browned. Serve warm with a Veggie Chilli (see p78), some GMVs (p52) or some veggie sausages and Black Bean Salsa (p39).

If you enjoyed the recipes in this book here are some other vegetarian recipes you'll find in my first book, *Beyond Baked Beans*:

EGGS
- Egyptian-style eggs with chickpeas
- Stirred eggs with chilli and coriander

PASTA
- Genoese pasta with pesto, potatoes and beans
- Penne with courgettes and lemon
- Ricotta and spinach tortellini with lemon butter sauce
- Tagliatelle with sweet tomato and fresh basil sauce ♣

SOUPS
- Chunky potato, onion and garlic soup ♣
- Hot chilli butternut squash soup
- Pea, broccoli and mint soup
- Real Thai cup-a-soup ♣
- Three-can chilli bean soup

SALADS
- Moroccan spiced carrot salad ♣
- Ultimate potato salad
- Warm pepper salad ♣

SNACKS
- Cottage cheese, garlic and coriander naan
- Garlic mushrooms on toast
- Grilled ciabatta with mozzarella, cherry tomatoes and pesto drizzle
- Italian bread 'pizza'
- Nachos
- Stuffed pitta breads with felafel, salad and garlicky yoghurt dressing

VEGGIE MAINS
- Chilean corn pie
- Classic macaroni cheese
- Creamy garlic and potato bake
- Light leeks with creamy Dolcelatte sauce
- New potato and green bean balti
- Spiced sweet potato, pepper and aubergine bake
- Thai tofu, sweetcorn and sugarsnap pea curry
- Truffled mushroom risotto
- Vegetable samosa pie

VEGGIE SIDES
- Creamy beans with garlic ♣
- Hot buttered sprouts with almonds
- Tarka dhal with crispy onions ♣
- Wokked roast potatoes ♣

DIPS AND RELISHES
- Cheat's hummus
- Chimichurri salsa ✿
- Red-hot pineapple salsa ✿

BREADS
- Good old-fashioned garlic bread
- Quick garlic flatbreads

SWEET THINGS
- Brown sugar bananas
- Cardamom rice pudding with shaved mango
- Cheat's Christmas pudding
- Fresh tropical fruit with mango sorbet
- Frosted berries with white chocolate and cardamom sauce
- Good old-fashioned apple crumble
- Iced pavlovas with fresh orange and passion fruit sauce
- Iced vodka and lemon sorbet
- Liquid summer pudding
- Pan-fried apple with honey, lemon and ginger ✿
- Smashed strawberry meringue
- Warm apple and cinnamon compote ✿
- Warm plum and rum tart
- Wicked chocolate sauce

DRINKS
- Caipirinha • Daiquiri • Mango lassi
- Margarita • Mojito • Rum punch
- Sea breeze • White sangria

WWW.BEYONDBAKEDBEANS.COM

There's also the website, which was recently listed by the *Independent* as one of the top 50 websites for foodies, and among the 8 best for 'recipes, chat and reference'. You can find regular updates and new recipes there. Take a look. If you want to contribute a recipe or share a tip, e-mail me: fiona@beyondbakedbeans.com

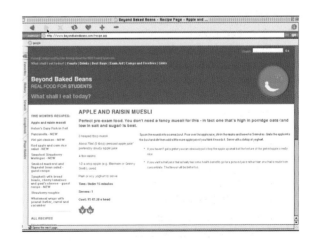

THANKS TO...

Thanks to all my veggie friends who have given me the benefit of their advice, especially Sean Dooley, who passed on the products and dishes he couldn't live without. To my long-suffering family, for their patience and support, particularly my husband Trevor who uncomplainingly (well, almost) survived without meat for weeks. And Will, Jo, Kate and Flyn, who didn't have to but were there in spirit. (Thanks Flyn for insisting that the cover should be green.) To Jon, Meg and Matt at Absolute – you were great as always (now where's the cheque?). To Andy, for the fantastic images. To Meg Devenish, for the lowdown on student shopping habits. To John, Sean (again) and Helen, for keeping the website going. And to Leigh, for making the world aware of both it and the book.

ABOUT THE AUTHOR

Fiona Beckett has been a student (twice) and has also been on the receiving end of endless calls from her four children – which still go on now – about how to cook everthing from cheese on toast to risotto. She's also an award-winning journalist who has written for most of the national press from the *People* to the *Financial Times*. She currently writes on food and drink for *Sainsbury's Magazine*, is contributing editor to the wine magazine *Decanter* and runs two websites, including the website of this book, www.beyondbakedbeans.com. All of which leaves not nearly enough time to spend with her long-suffering friends and family or following the fortunes of Liverpool Football Club.